Advanced Quilting

Elsie Svennås

Translated from the Swedish
by Richard and Lena Fleming

Charles Scribner's Sons
New York

Published by Charles Scribner's Sons New York

1 3 5 7 9 11 13 15 17 19 Q/C 20 18 16 14 12 10 8 6 4 2

Printed in the United States of America
Library of Congress Catalog Card Number
79-93151

ISBN 0-684-16612-7

Contents

FOREWORD

Since writing my last book on patchwork I have
continued my work within this field but with more
emphasis on quilting, and I have been experimenting
with various sewing techniques and ways of using
quilting. Ideas have often come to me quite accidentally.
For example, on one occasion I was planning to sew a
coverlet and experimented first by making a pot-holder
to try joining pieces together and quilting at the same
time. When I noticed that the pot-holder looked like a
stage, I made a larger version of it as a "wall-theatre". A
round flat table intended to be sewn on to the "stage"
had its edge damaged, so I made a pot-holder out of it, in
the form of a face with a hat to hide the damaged edge. If
the loop had not been made from red terry-towelling, I
would probably never have thought of pulling it through
the button-hole-like mouth like a tongue. It became a
pot-holder that could be attached to a hot handle, or a
glasses case – the face also had glasses. Stimulated by
this break, I set to work and made the coverlet that had
been the cause of all this. I hope my readers will also be
able to make exciting discoveries as a result of ap-
proaching the work in this playful spirit.

Elsie Svennås

ACKNOWLEDGEMENTS

TECHNICAL ADVICE Elsie and Ulla Svennås.
DESIGNS Four waistcoats p. 52, "Cinema" p. 69,
patchwork square p. 23, glasses case p. 35, ox-eye daisies
p. 37, bag and poncho p. 38, elephants p. 42, jacket p. 47,
square-patterned waistcoat p. 55, rug and triangular
cushion p. 61, bench cushion p. 62, bag p. 88, tablecloth
and insert p. 89, doll p. 130, Gunila Strömbäck. Flower-
patterned bag p. 70 and face mask p. 133, Louise Öquist.
Leaves p. 37, Cecilia Andersson. Embroidered waistcoat
p. 53, Ritva Hansson. Child's waistcoat p. 53, Bitte
MacLean. Waistcoat p. 82, Agot Fauske. "Shingle
beach" p. 119, Margareta Lundsten. Flying bird p. 121
and positive/negative image p. 102, Christina Wisting.
Window p. 129, Maria Yourstone. Hobby-horse p. 130,
Lena Carlén. Globe artichoke p. 120 and chair seat p. 27,
Ulla Svennås. Pig p. 120, Ann-Marie Forsberg. Puzzle
p. 132, Lotta Lindwall. Finger puppets p. 66 and 72, Eva
Billow. The lace figures are from Czechoslovakia and
the single doll in one of the illustrations on p. 66 is from
Mexico. The detail of old quilting on p. 40 is from the
Nordic Museum, Stockholm. Complete quilts and details from Bryce Hamilton's collections have been used
on the following pages: 4, 8, 17, 19–24, 28, 29, 32, 50, 51, 102
and also the lumberjacket on p. 52, the bag on p. 34 and
the small joined cushions on p. 43. Otherwise, where no
other origin is mentioned in the text, Elsie Svennås.
PHOTOGRAPHS Sirkka Lehtonen, Won Oh and Rys-
zard Jakubiak. Exceptions: pp. 36 and 37, Sven-Eric
Sjöström, leaves p. 37 and puzzle p. 132, Lucien Szczucki.
DRAWINGS Elsie Svennås.

WHAT IS QUILTING?

Quilting is sewing several layers of cloth together, usually with an insulating middle layer. The word quilt has been used since the thirteenth century.

Quilting, often combined with appliqué work and patchwork, has a long history of use by various peoples, and of adaptation to suit differing conditions, as can be seen from museum collections. Originally a practical device to make clothes both warm and soft, quilting's decorative function came later. The Chinese are said to have been the first to use quilting, but there is also a fine old tradition in India, Persia and the Islamic areas of Africa.

In Europe the technique was used in the Middle Ages; quilted jackets, for example, were used as protection beneath soldiers' coats of mail and suits of armour. Quilting flourished during the seventeenth century; England and Italy became famous for their beautiful quilted work, sometimes called *matelassé* from the French *matelas*, meaning mattress.

Patchwork quilts became a speciality in North America, where the emigrants used scraps of material and worn-out clothes that they had taken over with them, and many patterns were evolved. Such quilts are of great historical and cultural importance, and are highly valued by collectors.

In Scandinavia padded coverlets have been in use since the sixteenth century, originally for ornament and later mainly for warmth. The simpler ones were made of hand-woven cloth, and those in upper-class homes were often of silk. It is difficult to be certain about the part played by emigrants returning home from America in the development of Swedish patchwork quilts.

At present there is a lot of interest in quilting. Quilted jackets and other quilted items are becoming more

Many of the old patterns are still being used. Details can be copied for a variety of uses. This is a detail from a common quilting pattern in both patchwork and appliqué work.

Quilting is most attractive when it lies in natural folds. The illustrations in this book are mainly to show patterns and ways of working. It is very difficult to express in an illustration the tactile dimension that one experiences while sewing.

Surfaces and lines of machine quilting are decorative and add strength. The edge of a hat from West Africa, sewn on a simple treadle machine. Three colours on white.

common, and it is possible to buy ready-quilted material. Artists and craftsmen all over the world are increasingly turning to textiles in order, as it were, to sculpt in cloth, often using techniques which come under the heading of quilting. Any image, whether representational or abstract, has more life than a completely flat picture if it has light and shaded areas and gradations of colour.

HOW IS IT DONE?

In principle, two layers of cloth and a middle layer of filling are fastened together, but there are various techniques, such as knotting, sewing either by hand or on a machine, and embroidery. The work may be done quickly, or it may be very time-consuming. Generations of skilful and resourceful women have, with much patience and feeling for material, worked out practical solutions by trial and error. There is not room for everything in a book such as this, but the potential for further development is enormous once you know the basic principles. This book is intended to inspire you to be creative. Advice and practical tips are included in the captions to the illustrations.

Experimenting with quilting can be a lot of fun as well as giving you valuable experience of materials and of both hand and machine sewing. Don't start off with over-ambitious projects. If things go wrong, try to make the best of the situation. I have often had good ideas as the result of doing this. My aim is to stimulate you to re-use material and to use what you have to hand. Using such materials, you can afford to make a few mistakes.

One advantage of quilting is that it doesn't need ironing, so long as the cloth used is sufficiently smooth to begin with. In most kinds of sewing, seams are pressed as the work goes along. If you quilt at the same time as you sew the pieces together, pressing becomes unnecessary. Often the filling, for example flannel, felt or knitted wool, will not stand up to being pressed. It is better to allow the material to form itself naturally as the work progresses. In traditional quilting the top fabric is usually completed in either patchwork or appliqué work, either entire or in manageable blocks, before the filling and the backing materials are put in place behind it and the whole thing is quilted. It may be advisable with this kind of work either to press or to stretch out the top fabric.

If a piece of quilting is to be lined, edged or attached to a smooth piece of cloth, the raised portions of the quilting should be evenly distributed and held in place with pins and tacking. Otherwise it may wrinkle and pucker when it is sewn.

Quilting is often made reversible. The side which is facing up when the quilting is being stitched is called the top fabric in the text. It may have a printed or a woven pattern to help with the quilting, or the pattern may be traced, drawn or scratched on with a needle. One method is to stitch along the edge of a paper template fastened temporarily or held in place by hand. In appliqué work and patchwork, the quilting often follows the shapes of the pieces.

Securing the ends of a large number of threads is very time-consuming, and sewing cotton is expensive. Avoid it by quilting in patterns which do not require so many breaks. Long straight runs of stitching are the easiest, cutting out the need to twist and turn the work, though some kinds of material stretch too much on long runs. Sometimes this can be used to produce quilting with a kind of herringbone effect, which also makes it warmer. If the stitching is at too frequent intervals, the thick and open-textured filling becomes compressed and thin – sturdy but not so warm.

A cross-section of a piece of quilting shows how the cloth is raised between the stitching by the filling, thus using extra material. It is safest to allow yourself some margin, and to trim when you have finished quilting. Some types of material are stiff and unresponsive, others soft and elastic. If the top and bottom layers are of similar weights, the raised portions will be equal on both sides. If you want a smooth side and a raised one, choose your materials accordingly.

If a surface is to be quilted using straight, parallel lines of stitching, the ridges will be soft and attractive if the grain of both layers of cloth is laid in the same direction and the quilting is stitched on the bias. If the quilting is stitched in the same direction as the weave, the result may pucker, though this is not necessarily undesirable. If two pieces of cloth are to be joined together or with a layer of filling, stretching along the seams may be

Cross-section of equal-sided

and unequal-sided quilting.

Quilting on the bias.

One piece of fabric laid out and one on the bias helps to prevent stretching.

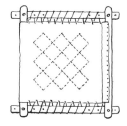

Large items are rolled up to facilitate machine sewing.

Quilting frame with tape nailed on and (left) oval frame made in America, larger than a normal embroidery frame and complete with a stand.

If a thin material is attached to a knitted fabric or other type of fabric that is under tension, the result when the tension is removed is a bubbly, elastic texture.

avoided by laying the grain of each in different directions, fabric with the grain laid straight next to fabric in which the grain is laid diagonally. This is effective not only with straight stitching and seams but also, for example, when joining together two circular pieces of material.

If large pieces of work are to be quilted by machine, they should first be pinned or tacked to keep the layers of cloth in place. Often it may be necessary to roll up parts of the work in order to pass it through the machine, possibly with some assistance.

Small pieces, and in exceptional cases large pieces, can be quilted while hand-held or spread out on a table, but the result will be better if a frame is used. Quilting frames made out of four pieces of wood can be bought or made. It is possible to make use of old picture or window frames. Ordinary round embroidery frames or square ones made up of four strips of wood, metal or plastic, or frames intended for machine embroidery, are suitable for smaller pieces of work.

CHOOSING MATERIAL

When you know how to quilt it is easier to choose your material. All types of cloth can be used, but they behave differently and have different applications. The top fabric is chosen for its appearance, the filling to give strength and insulation and to lift up the top fabric, and the backing to form a soft lining or to give firm support to emphasize the relief of the top fabric. Many people think that the pieces in patchwork should be of exactly the same weight, and certainly in, say, a quilt the pieces should be fairly similar. But often it is the difference in structure which provides the effect, and in some cases the colour of the material is more important than the quality.

The filling generally helps to hold the quilt's shape, but

it should be chosen with regard to the way the quilt is to be used and handled, since it will seldom be possible to iron it; consider whether or how it is to be washed, and whether it will shrink or its colours run etc.

Even if you prefer natural fibres, synthetic fibres are often better. The cap on p. 43, for example, would not retain its fluffy shape if it were not made of synthetic material, and pre-quilted nylon lining is very useful and durable.

It is easy to mark out patterns on some materials, but with others it is quite impossible. Some require a large seam allowance, others fray and slip. In general, thin cotton material is easy to work with and many types such as muslin and satin give the work an attractive sheen. Soft and elastic materials such as jersey, elasticated terry-towelling and knitted materials produce a very soft relief but are difficult to sew on a machine.

Soft leather is very attractive when quilted. The elasticity of this material can be used in various ways, such as *trapunto* quilting and padded appliqué work, see pp. 19, 40, 41, 42, 75, and 143. Leather is easily damaged when pinning, tacking and unpicking, but with care and practice it is possible to do various kinds of work with good results.

The filling, which cannot, of course, be seen in the illustrations, can be of down, wool, batting, felt, flannel, terry-towelling or some open-textured synthetic material. If it is thick it is called padding or stuffing irrespective of the technique used.

Down is light, warm, soft, but difficult to work with. It gets everywhere when being used to fill pre-sewn compartments and channels. The material used must be completely down-proof.

Wool is easier to handle, warm, and does not compact like cotton batting. It should be picked clean, washed and carded. An old woollen blanket or jumper makes an excellent filling, but it is advisable to pre-shrink it in hot water.

Old-fashioned cotton batting has been replaced by synthetic batting sold either by length or by weight. It can be used double, or the layers can be carefully separated. It starts off fluffy but compresses to almost nothing where stitched, or if the quilting is too close together. This can be an advantage when quilting by hand, as a lot of stitches may be gathered on the needle before it is drawn through. Synthetic batting is fairly translucent, and is therefore suitable for lampshades and window ornaments. Old nylon stockings are good in certain cases for padding and filling.

Flannel gives stability and does not slip easily. It can be combined with an open-textured filling if necessary, Flannel tends to stick to things, and when several layers

of cloth move together it can be an advantage if the surfaces are rough. Felt, especially of the type used to protect table-tops, gives good heat-insulation.

Felt, flannel, terry-towelling, fur, artificial fur such as that used to make teddy-bears, and knitted and crocheted materials can be used as combined filling and backing.

Use strong thread and large-headed pins. Make sure that they are not left behind in the filling or sewn in between layers of cloth. Try sewing-needles of various lengths. Usually short needles are best.

USES FOR QUILTING

CLOTHES AND ACCESSORIES for both everyday use and special occasions can be quilted. Quilted clothes and bags are practical, can easily be made reversible and don't need ironing. If filled with synthetic batting they are also light. These are important advantages, especially when travelling.

The quilted clothing worn by the nobility in the eighteenth century, and Swedish leisure-clothing and folk-costumes, illustrate how successfully the technique may be adapted to suit differing needs or fashions, from simple, comfortable clothes to a more tailored look and to suit almost everyone.

Clothes which have been torn, become too small or boring can be re-used by means of appliqué work, patchwork and quilting.

Ready-to-wear quilted jackets can give you a lot of ideas about how and where to pad and join leather, cloth and knitted materials.

FURNISHINGS that are both warm and soft, in the home and in public places, can be quilted. The technique is suitable for all types of surroundings, both simple and exclusive. As a wall-hanging, quilting gives a cosy impression as well as helping sound-insulation. The work can easily be shared by members of a family or a group, each of whom can either do different stages of the work or do complete blocks which are later joined together.

Toys and cuddly playthings can also be quilted, and the technique is ideal as a vehicle for teaching exercises in composition, use of colour and the reproduction of images using three-dimensional effects.

QUILTS – BASIC TECHNIQUES

USING A QUILTING FRAME Cotton cloth is ideal for quilts. The top fabric may or may not be patterned, and may be decorated with appliqué work or made up of patches sewn together. The backing is selected according to whether the quilt is to be reversible or not. It is the filling which determines how warm and light the quilt will be. Wool washed clean and spread out gives a warm and fluffy quilt. For a thinner one you can use a worn blanket, terry-towelling or flannel. Synthetic batting is best if you want a light machine-washable quilt.

Quilting is easiest if you use a frame. This usually consists of two long and two short pieces of wood which stretch the quilt out while you are working on it. They are held in place at each corner by means of clamps or pegs. The principle is the same as that of a loom – as the work is quilted it is rolled from one piece of wood on to another. The short sides are the ones that are moved.

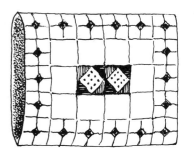

To quilt a whole bedspread without a quilting frame, it is easiest to sew the complete cover, carefully insert the filling, and lay the bedspread out on a table or the floor in order to quilt it.

Quilting frames can have legs, or be laid on trestles, chairs or tables, and may sometimes be held in place with clamps. Pin or tack from the centre.

Strong double thread is passed vertically up and down through material and filling. The ends are tied together in pairs.

First attach the long edges of the backing to the frame, followed by one of the long edges of the facing. Spread out the filling as evenly as possible on top of the backing and attach the facing to the other long side of the frame, and the piece which is to be quilted first is then stretched out by means of the short sides of the frame. Some people prefer to start from the centre, others from one of the long edges. Pin and tack. Mark out the pattern if necessary.

If you want quick results, or if the filling is very thick, threads can be drawn through and secured with reef knots. A knotted quilt is warmer than a stitched quilt. It is more usual, however, to quilt using small running stitches. Hold one hand below the quilt. If the stitches become too uneven, unpick them; it is no use trying to thread the needle back through. Use strong thread and secure it carefully without visible knots. Back-stitch, stem-stitch and chain-stitch produce a more even line but take longer. Make only one stitch at a time. If the material is striped, checked or boldly patterned, it is useful to quilt along the lines of the pattern. Otherwise guide-lines are necessary.

EMBROIDERY, APPLIQUÉ WORK Various types of embroidery may be used instead of quilting to hold the cloth and the filling together. To avoid having to mark out the pattern, choose material which can itself guide you; for example, sew cross-stitch on a fine check. If you also choose terry-towelling as the backing, filling will not be necessary and the quilting will be easy even without a frame. The stitches are invisible on the reverse of terry-towelling. Another method is to sew on small patches, crocheted stars or stars made out of binding or ribbon, using stitches that run right through the quilt. This gives the same effect as the buttons on a mattress. These stars and patches can also be used for matching decorations on the sheets.

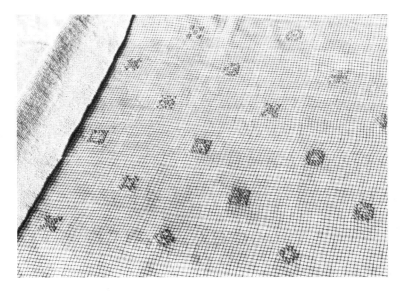

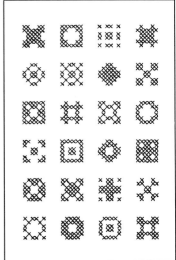

Patterns for the quilt on the left.

Stars made from ribbons or binding. Fold the two ends alternately into the middle until the hexagon is complete, cut off, push in and fasten the corners.

If both facing and backing are striped they are laid with the grain of each at right-angles to the other and the quilting which follows the stripes of one runs at right-angles across the other. If the edging strip is to be sewn on afterwards then two edges are sewn from one side and two from the other.

QUILTING WITH A SEWING MACHINE

It is of course quicker to sew with a machine than by hand, but a complete quilt is rather unmanageable. It is easier to quilt blocks which are then sewn together. Straight stitching is most commonly used, but you can use zig-zag stitching, which is more elastic and therefore stronger when used, for example, on a very elastic material. If the machine is set to the narrowest zig-zag, the result will look like straight stitching.

It is quite easy to get used to handling the work in such a way that the cloth and the filling can be fed smoothly through the machine at the same time, but it is as well to pin or tack thoroughly at first. It helps to lessen the tension on the presser foot. If the material still tends to be pushed forwards, take out the pins and correct the distortion. Check from time to time that there are no creases in the backing. If the lines of stitching cross, the facing can easily become puckered because of the machine's tendency to push the material along in front of it.

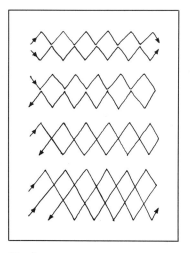

Various ways of quilting diamond shapes.

Closely-stitched quilting produces a lower relief, greater stability and a less warm quilt than quilting with the stitching further apart. Think about the order and the direction in which the quilting should be sewn. It is difficult to turn the work frequently and inconvenient to have to secure a lot of ends. Sometimes it may be best only to sew in one direction, sometimes to sew backwards and forwards. One way of forming a pattern of diamond shapes is to sew in zig-zag lines, as shown in the illustration. The material will pull out of shape more during long runs of sewing. Sometimes it may be a good plan to quilt squares using top fabric and filling and sew these together at the same time as they are sewn on to the backing.

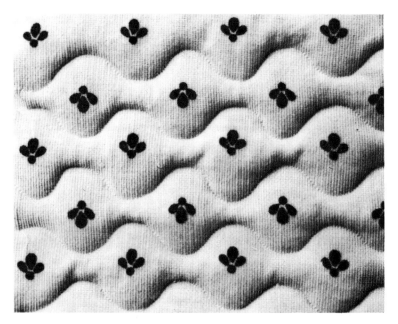

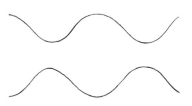

The wavy lines on the left and the curves below were sewn along the edges of templates, which, when pressed down on the material, also help to stop it puckering.

QUILTING PATTERNED MATERIALS such as stripes, checks and other patterns. It is easy to follow stripes in materials, and it is also possible to sew by eye from point to point (see below). Another method is to use a paper template aligned with the printed pattern. A transparent template is even better. Attach it temporarily with pins or hold it in place by hand, moving it as required. Large pattern shapes are easily followed using a sewing machine; smaller shapes may be best sewn by hand. Experiment with different quilting patterns on the same material; for example, on blocks used to make up a quilt. As the illustrations show, this can produce quite a range of effects.

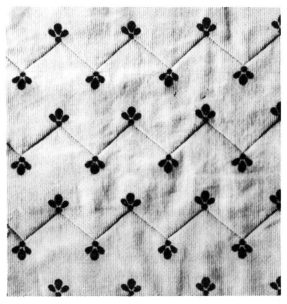

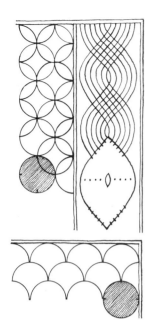

It is easier to fit in a template or a circular object if the edges have been marked in. Wavy lines which cross each other can be drawn in by hand with the help of small dots made through the holes and the cuts in the edges of the template.

Sometimes dotted lines are best.

MARKING OUT PATTERNS

LINES, RECTANGLES, GEOMETRIC PATTERNS
Straight lines can be marked on to fabric by folding, with sticky tape (which should be removed as soon as possible) or by snapping a chalked line. Marks can be made along the edge of a ruler or of templates cut from cardboard or plastic, using a pencil, tailor's chalk or by scratching with the point of a needle. Dotted lines are more easily hidden by the stitching than are unbroken lines. The choice of method will depend on the material, the method of sewing and how clear you want the markings to be. The pattern can be marked out in full from the start, or bit by bit. Markings can be made so faint that they disappear by themselves. To mark circular shapes, use glasses, plates, cups or a pair of compasses.

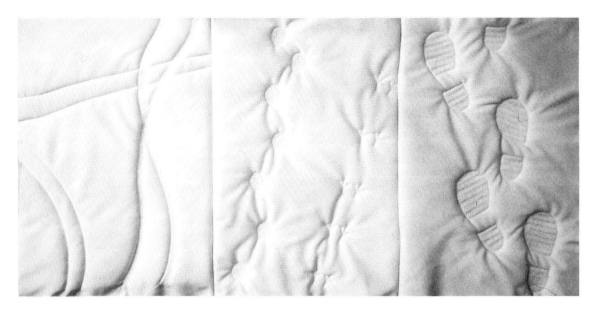

FREE PATTERNS Rhythmic lines can be drawn freehand with a pencil or a needle directly on to the material. You can also draw with a pencil round a leaf, an outspread hand or a foot. The quilts on this page show tracks made by people and animals in snow (above) and sand (below). You can go outside and copy tracks in snow and sand, or draw them from memory. It is also easy to make imprints and transfer them on to your material. The quilting can be done by machine or by hand, either in one piece or in blocks which are later sewn together. A clean, fresh quilt with such a snow design is delightfully inviting in the middle of summer, while in winter the quilt showing tracks in sand is a reminder of summer. If you want the tracks to look as if they have sunk into the material, it is not sufficient to stitch only round the outlines of the paws, feet or hooves. You must devise some method of holding down the surface inside these outlines – see the cat tracks above and the footmarks. The technique used in the bottom centre block could also be used to represent rope.

Synthetic white jersey on both sides of synthetic batting looks like snow. The tracks are sewn by machine using movable paper templates. Straight and zig-zag stitching with as few ends as possible.

Sand-coloured Indian cotton with synthetic filling. Experiment with hand stitching, for outlines and surfaces. Above, a way of sewing a rope, for example.

VERY DETAILED QUILTING all over a coverlet is extremely demanding work. It is easier if you use continuous filling, but there is a variant called *trapunto*, which originated in Italy, in which the filling is inserted into the shapes that form the pattern. It is used more for ornament than for warmth.

These illustrations show samples of very demanding techniques. Above, a quilt which probably has a continuous thin filling, and on the right a quilt with padding within stitched outlines. The quilt is old and the filling tightly packed, and obviously the ridges have always been under strain. The quilting of the background plays a very minor role in the design.

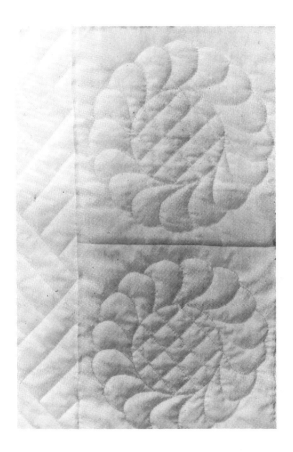

From the seventeenth century onwards magnificent quilts and even clothes were made in England using the techniques illustrated on page 19. The patterns were made up of stylized flowers, leaves, fruits and feathers, against a closely quilted background. The patterns were carefully drawn on to the top or the bottom of the quilt with the help of templates made of pewter or cardboard. These techniques spread to the U.S.A., especially the southern states, and beautiful quilts in this style have also survived in Sweden.

The technique has become simplified over the years; instead of cotton, linen or silk, synthetic textiles are often used, both for the coverings and the fillings, and the stitching is often done by machine. The results are quite different – compare the illustrations on page 19 with those above – and lack the feeling of heaviness of the older quilts. Templates like those illustrated can be bought in England and America, and it is not difficult to cut them out yourself from thin, stiff cardboard. Complete quilts, hand-sewn in the traditional way with rich patterns such as those shown here, are seldom made nowadays, but it is possible to use this technique to sew cushions, glasses-cases, small squares for making cases or holders, decorations for clothes and so on. Stretch out the work using a frame, tack carefully and sew with small, even stitches.

A newly-made quilt in modern materials looks quite different.

The quilt on the far right is shown in colour on p. 51. The other one has blue stripes and red stars on a white background. The quilting often follows the seams to give extra strength.

20

Fold paper, or even cloth, backwards and forwards so that the fold becomes thinner, otherwise the pattern may be irregular. Here the edge is cut away.

Sometimes the centre is cut away.

MIXING TECHNIQUES

One way of giving the work a little variety while also gaining experience of various techniques is to sew and join together blocks of appliqué work, patchwork and plain quilting. The quilt above has strips of finely patterned and quilted material, which gives the design unity. Appliqué work can be used on a quilted background and be given extra padding to emphasize the relief. Patterns for appliqué work can be cut out of folded paper. Patterns such as these, often large enough to cover the entire quilt, are typical of Hawaii.

*Quilt with different repre-
sentational motifs, all facing in the same direction.*

*Details of the quilt on the
left are shown on p. 4.*

A pattern can be repeated using different techniques on
the same quilt. Flower motifs can be used in all manner
of ways – as large central medallions, in equal-sized
blocks with different motifs all facing in the same
direction; or spread all over the surface of the quilt. In
the illustration (above) the flowers appear to have been
picked from around the edge and arranged in vases. The
design might have had more spontaneity if they had
been cut out in a wider variety of shapes. An easy way
often used to achieve a richer pattern is to cut the shapes
out of patterned chintzes or oriental fabrics. The areas
between the bunches of flowers are discreetly quilted,
almost certainly after the completion of the appliqué
work. For more details on appliqué work, see later
sections of this book.

*The shapes and colours of
the patches, the quilting
and the embroidery, all
contribute different effects
to the pattern.*

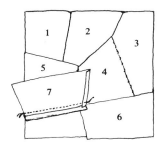

Lay the right sides facing each other, and sew by hand or by machine until the block is full. Open edges can be folded in and fastened with concealed stitching afterwards, or with zig-zag stitching or embroidery.

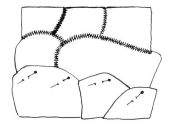

Patches can also be placed fairly haphazardly and quilted into place with zig-zag stitching or suitable embroidery.

SEWING PATCHES TOGETHER

One way of using scraps of material is to leave their shapes more or less as they are and to sew them one after the other on to backing material of the required size and thickness. This is called crazy quilting in America. Pieces which are light and dark, patterned and plain, are combined to form a whole. On older quilts the seams are strengthened and decorated with embroidery and sometimes names, dates and small design motifs. This is a good way of using up scraps of embroidered material and other expensive fabrics, and it can be used for other items as well as quilts.

Small and apparently haphazardly arranged patches are seen on closer inspection to be arranged in lines radiating from the centre, and then one suddenly realizes that the entire quilt is made up of diamond shapes, all the same size and all made of strips of material sewn together. The whole coverlet was then filled and quilted in a diagonal pattern.

Typical Victorian quilt with squares and borders. Some of the patches were already embroidered, others were decorated with small embroidered motifs.

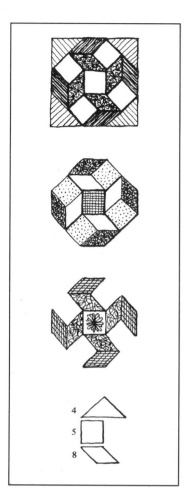

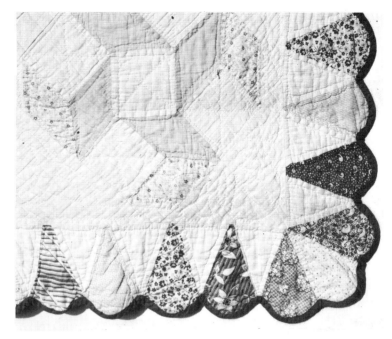

Traditional American patchwork design. Above, as a complete square, and an octagon as a millwheel. Below, the number of each patch required to make a square, with their shapes and relative sizes.

JOINING LARGE BLOCKS It is easier to work with small blocks than with whole quilts. Each member of a group can sew a block from start to finish, even quilting it. It is essential to make them all exactly the same size. They can then be stitched together by hand or laid edge to edge and the join covered with binding. Another method is to place the blocks face to face and sew along the edge by machine, later covering the seam with binding or strips of material. There are both simple and laborious methods. If you can get hold of a quilting frame, it is perhaps best to join the blocks together before quilting the whole coverlet. The edge is very important. It may sometimes be so simple that it is quite unobtrusive, and sometimes form an important element of the design. It is often said that borders and corners are the greatest test of one's skill in designing patterns. The border above contrasts very effectively with the rest of the design.

Edge to edge.   Face to face.   One edge of the material over the seam.

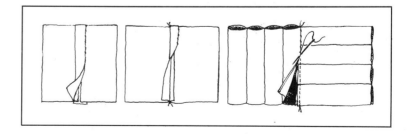

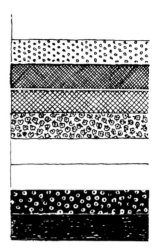

JOINING SMALL PIECES There are many ways of joining small four-sided pieces to form long lengths or whole pieces. Using long strips of cloth, it is easy to join them to form a striped piece, then to cut at right-angles to the seams, move these strips along by one or more places, and sew the edges together again. This can be done very quickly using a machine. If the machine has a special stitch for sewing the flies and seats of trousers then use it; it will not come undone when you cut across the seam. The cutting, moving along and sewing together is repeated according to a system. An example of the result of this technique is shown in colour on p. 49

Strips of cloth sewn together to make a square-patterned quilt. Notice the rhythm of the dark and light, plain and finely patterned patches.

The quilting can be done later or at the same time as you sew the pieces together. In the latter case, the strips cut from the piece made up of long strips are then sewn row after row on to the filling and the backing. If you want quilting running in different directions, this is done afterwards. The quilt shown above is made of layers joined together by a couple of small stitches in the corners of each square. The resulting coverlet is airy and warm but does not look as if it is quilted.

You can sew together and quilt at the same time, and produce ridges in high or low relief.

MOSAICS of triangles, rectangles and hexagons joined together can be varied endlessly. The illustrations show

Following the principle described above, pieces of material made up from strips sewn together in various ways, to look like folds, plaits, herringbone patterns or even spirals. Generally the angle is the same throughout. On a large scale, patterns of this type are suitable for curtains and hangings, on a smaller scale for curtain pelmets and borders and edges.

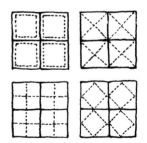

Four examples of ways of quilting surfaces built up from joined squares, preferably by hand.

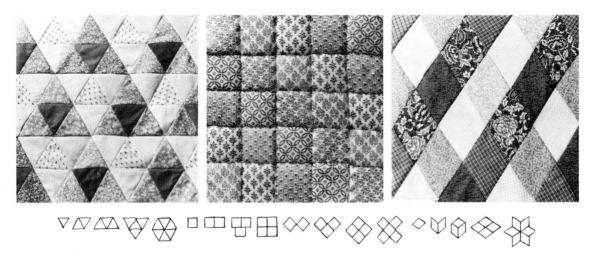

Be careful with sharp angles. Cut away the actual point and fold the material as neatly as possible around the edge of the template.

It is also possible to sew the pieces together with the right sides facing along the edge of a template pinned in position.

how basic designs can grow into larger designs, and how pyramids, lattice-work, brick walls and stylized flights of birds are built up. All of these, except the hexagons, are sewn together and quilted at the same time, using a sewing machine. Some of the seams in the piece shown at top left are hand sewn. Choose patterned materials which suit the sizes of the patches. Cut them out, using a template made of card or transparent plastic, leaving a seam allowance. The materials may be laid with the grain running in various directions, as the backing helps to stop the quilt pulling out of shape. The patches are first sewn together into strips, for example, or into squares or triangles. Use the simplest method available.

A special method of joining hexagons is shown below, and this can also be used for other shapes. This commonly used way of joining patches is time-consuming but produces very good results.

The sides of a hexagon = the radius of a circle. Accurately cut templates are covered with the cloth folded round the edges and pressed, taped, tacked or stitched at each corner. Sew together by hand or using machine zig-zag either edge to edge or with right sides facing each other. The templates are removed when no longer required. Right, round shape made from hexagons.

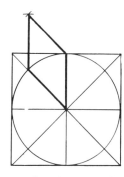

The angle of an equilateral template.

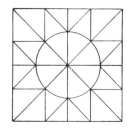

Continue the pattern as shown here to make the star.

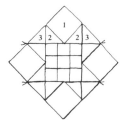

Following the order shown by the numbers, all the patches can be sewn together by machine. First three sections.

LARGE AND SMALL STARS Triangles, diamonds and hexagons can be joined together to form several types of star. The patterns shown here are all built up of diamond shapes, all the sides of which are of equal length. The angle is obtained by folding a piece of paper as shown at top right. The patches used to make the pot-holder and the quilt shown in colour on p. 51 are sewn together by machine, including the squares and the triangles. This is done by sewing them together face-to-face. To get the angle, the work is turned round the needle of the sewing machine in the same way as when sewing binding on to the edge of a square. The corners of the pot-holder are patterned, which seems to give the star perspective. On the quilt all of the eight pieces of cloth around the star are of finely patterned material. Two pieces of another material make the star into a flower. The quilting of the pot-holders exactly follows the pressed seams between the patches. The quilt will be fluffier if the squares are free of quilting. The bias-cut strips of material which join and cover the edges of the squares are attached by stitching that runs right through the filling and the backing. It is also possible just to sew on such strips to the top and backing fabrics and in this simple manner make a square-patterned quilt. The pattern above, "The Star of Bethlehem", starts as a small central star which is continued outwards using pieces of identical shape until the star is the size required. Round the star are large squares and triangles, quilted with a design of hearts. The centre of the quilt is shown in colour on p. 51.

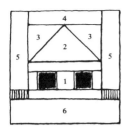

Diagram to show another way of joining patches to form a house. Start with rectangles for the windows and walls and continue outwards in the order shown by the numbers, entirely by machine.

Rows of houses, general view and detail. This shows patchwork, and also the way in which quilting can give a surface shape and life.

REPRESENTATIONAL MOTIFS on the blocks joined to form a quilt. It is easy to represent houses in patchwork. The quilt shown is probably most suitable as a wall-hanging; it looks like an estate of small detached houses. This is very suitable for group work; each member can be given the same house design, but chooses the materials and the colours used in each block.

Appliqué work and embroidery can be used to complete the picture. A possible variant would be to make a long row of houses with a street in front and gardens in between. Another example of a house design in patchwork is shown on the next page. It is a good idea to sew a trial square to test the design.

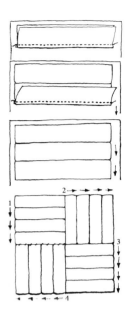

A variant of this technique it to work round as illustrated. The final edge is fastened with hidden stitching. Squares can be joined together to create a woven or plaited effect.

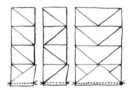

The method can also be adapted using triangles to make belts and borders.

SEWING AND FOLDING DOWN Place two pieces on the backing or on the backing and filling, with their right sides facing each other. Sew together along one edge and fold the top piece down on to the backing or filling. Repeat this process, which is an easy and enjoyable way of assembling and quilting at the same time. Usually parallel-sided pieces are used, but also occasionally tapering pieces. The evening bag on p. 35 was made this way. The technique can also be used to make belts, borders, and blocks for making into quilts and cushions.

If pot-holders or other squares are sewn together from strips which continue on the reverse and are folded down progressively, the open side and the lower edge can be sewn together afterwards by hand.

Wide strips sewn together can be quilted in stripes as shown on the right. The widths of the strips can also be varied.

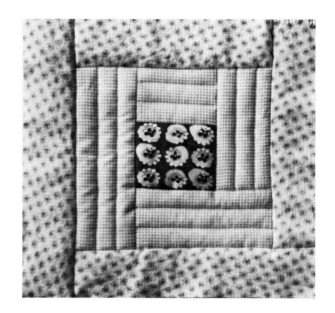

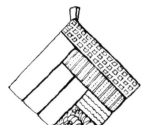

Houses can also be represented in this way. When making pot-holders, the strips can be taken round on to the reverse side.

SEWING AND FOLDING DOWN – IN TWO OR MORE DIRECTIONS This is a common patchwork technique of Canadian origin, called log-cabin because the result looks rather like logs laid at right-angles to each other.

Start with a square in the centre or corner of a square piece of backing, and sew on strip after strip following one of the designs shown on the next page. The most common method is to work round and round until the square is the required size. It is also possible to work alternately on opposite sides. The traditional patterns use light and dark pieces arranged as shown in the squares at top centre. The squares can be assembled horizontally as in the illustration on the right, or diagonally. Starting with a central square, you can sew on larger and larger triangles alternately straight and across the corners – see the second square from the right at the top of the opposite page.

A square sewn from corner to corner can look like a flower – pointing up or down – and be used to make a pot-holder, cushion, pocket or edging on, for example, a quilt.

A variant is to sew narrow strips together in this manner. If you use dark and light strips as shown in the square at top right, the result is a pattern called pineapple. If progressively darker or lighter pieces are sewn on as you work outwards, this gives an impression of depth. Ways of using the log-cabin technique to make representational designs are illustrated on pp. 65 and 66.

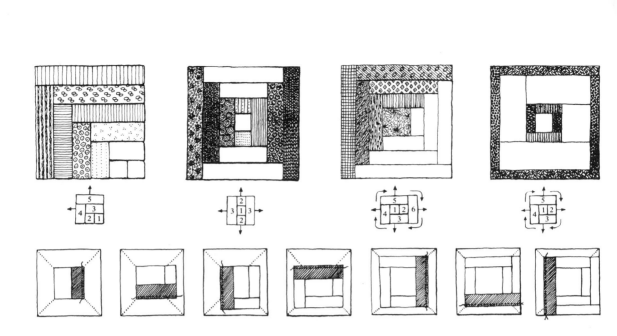

Start with a square (or whatever shape you choose) at the centre and mark out the diagonals. Strips and sometimes also triangles are then sewn in place, and folded down in the direction and order given.

Variations of sewing and folding down.

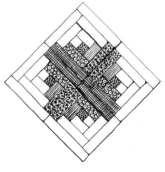

Quilt in log-cabin pattern.

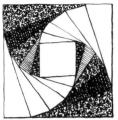 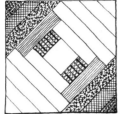 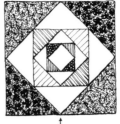 

Above: triangles joined to-gether, or appliqué on appliqué.

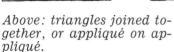

QUILTING – FURTHER USES, MORE TECHNIQUES

Much of what has been said about quilting, piecing together and patterns for quilts can be applied in other circumstances. Quilting is a useful way of protecting things, replacing things which have become worn, making unusual items and saving material. It may be a good way of covering a chair or a sofa, an expensive job if done by a professional. A delicate suede jacket may be improved by the addition of a detachable, washable collar and sleeve protectors. If you have an expensive and attractive woollen jersey that has for some reason become too small, it can be enlarged using quilted strips. You may well have saved buckles, handbag frames and other items in case they ever came in handy. This section of the book describes techniques and various ways of applying them. The results obtained will depend very largely on the materials used.

 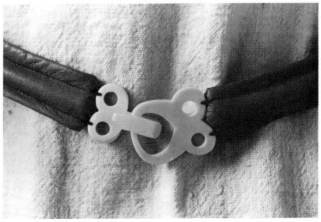

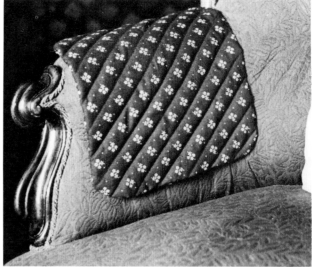

It is important to consider the uses to which objects will be put. Very thick fillings are mainly used for decorative objects and for things not washed in the normal way, such as wall hangings, upholstery on chairs and stools and so on. Various materials can be used. The items illustrated are mostly made of cloth, but leather is sometimes as good or better. If the quilting is mainly intended to produce a decorative relief pattern, light-coloured fabrics are most suitable. Finely patterned material can be quilted in all kinds of designs, whereas with boldly patterned material it is often better to emphasize the pattern by quilting around its outlines.

Sometimes a piece of work will have its own special technical problems which you will have to solve yourself. Materials, for example, may behave in different ways, and we may apply different standards to the results.

The toilet bag is made from the best bits of an old track-suit, with synthetic batting and a nylon lining, and a monogram in cotton material. The quilting around the appliqué runs right through and secures the inside pockets, an idea that can also be used on clothes.

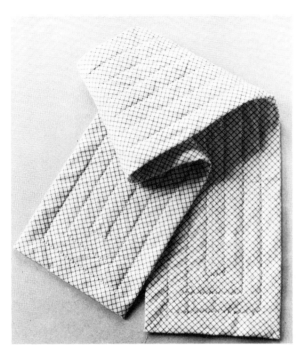

A felted scarf covered with soft, square-patterned material cut on the bias. Hand quilted with a stitch in each square.

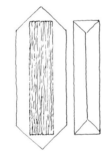

The illustrations show various materials and ways of sewing: a classic hand-bag in silk with silk stem-stitch on an old frame; an elegant evening bag or glasses-case made from linen patches sewn together; a sporty denim bag.

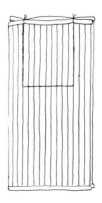

Denim shoulder-bag. Two quilted pieces with edging at each end sewn together to form a pocket, and the bottom halves of each then folded up and edged so that the two outer pockets and the loops for fastening the strap are formed at the same time.

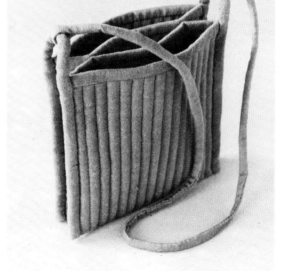

FOLLOW THE STRUCTURE-PATTERN OF THE
WEAVE Linen tablecloths and towels often have patterns which are ideal for quilting, and can be used to
make pot-holders, bags, ornaments for garments etc.
Pieces with differently patterned weaves can be sewn
together to make quilts, pillows and cushions, or even
wall-hangings such as the tiled stove shown on p. 134.

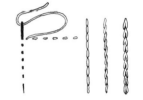

Various quilting stitches.

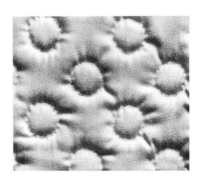

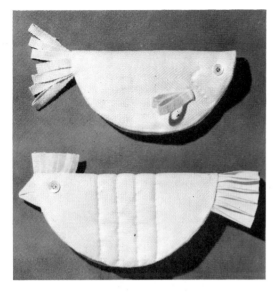

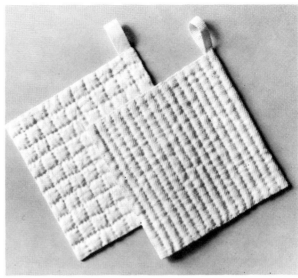

Round quilted shapes form a fish and a bird to slip over hot pan-handles.

Hand-printed material quilted so as to bring out the leaves' characteristic habit of growth.

QUILT THE PATTERN OF THE MATERIAL Small running stitches give a dotted effect typical of quilting. Back-stitch, stem-stitch and chain-stitch produce smoother lines. If the material has large unpatterned spaces, these may be quilted in squares, strips or wavy patterns, or with quilted motifs. The pieces of work illustrated here have filling below the entire surface. The quilting on the left was done by hand, that on the right by machine. Plain facing material can be quilted by means of a patterned backing.

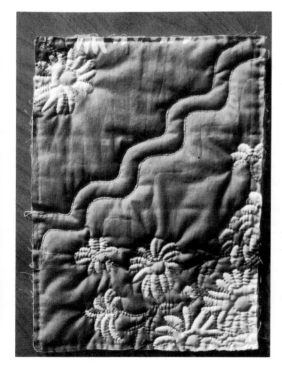

Left, neck opening of a quilted poncho made from a shawl.

An attempt to sew spirals by machine following a printed pattern became a baby chair. I used thin curtain material, synthetic batting and very thin jersey. The underside turned out to be more bubbly. I plan to use the idea again.

Belt or waistband of hand-woven cloth. Small running stitches for the stripes and stem-stitch round the geometrical shapes.

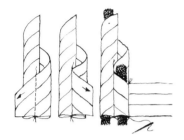

Edge with thick wool through two channels made from a single strip of material. Sewn on by machine with a seam down the middle, and concealed stitching on the underside.

PADDED EDGES around necklines, sleeves and skirts are decorative, give stability and strength, and can also be used to mend and to lengthen. Pulling through a strong cord will prevent stretching and help, for example, to shape a neckline. Bias binding or material with some elasticity is best, with the filling either put in first or pulled through afterwards. Strips of felted woollen material can be used sometimes as edging strips. Several strips or different coloured patterned ones can be added as required.

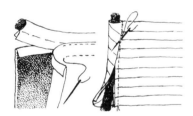

An edge can be sewn on or let in.

Child's skirt with a bodice meant to be tucked inside the skirt. Padded edge and fold which can be let out to increase both length and width. Allow for this in the initial length of the bodice and the waistband.

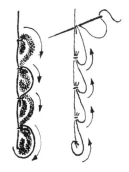

Cross-section of the edges on the left. Arrows show seams and direction of working. On the left felted wool, on the right velour.

FILLING BETWEEN QUILTING Below are shown old and new examples of the technique mentioned above, *trapunto* or *matelassé*. Using two layers of material, the lower of which is thin, parallel stitching is used to form tunnels which are filled with a thick woollen yarn. The fabrics can be laid with the grain running in different directions to prevent stretching. If necessary take the work out of the frame when pulling the yarn through. The yarn should be pre-shrunk and should be pulled through a little at a time to prevent it being put under tension and later shrinking, causing puckering. This is particularly important at curves and corners. Strips of knitted fabric can be used instead of woollen yarn, see below.

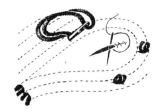

Pre-shrunk double wool on a blunt needle. Leave small loops, particularly at corners and curves. Stretch out the material so that loops work their way in.

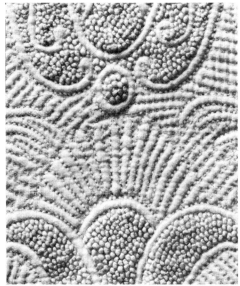

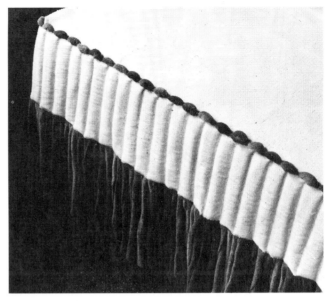

Elastic cloth and leather stretch over raised padded areas but remain smooth in between.

FILLING INSIDE QUILTED SHAPES is a variant of the technique which is described on the previous page. The pattern may be printed or drawn on the material. The filling can either be pushed in between the layers from the side before the sewing of the shape is finished, or

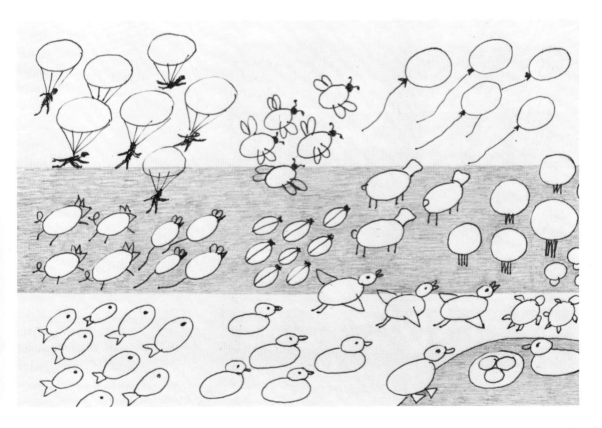

Top and underside of a piece of work in which small running stitches around the edges of round printed shapes join silk to a thin lining. Filling inserted in these round forms gives them shape, and daisy-stitch and small stalks make them into flowers or fruit. Try printing material yourself – perhaps using thumb-prints – or draw round an oval shape.

through small holes in the backing. These holes, which can be cut or formed by pushing the threads aside, should be sewn up afterwards. If thin material is used, this technique produces a shadowy effect. The picture on p. 41 shows water, land and air and appropriate living creatures in the form of round shapes in relief.

SEWING SMALL PADDED CUSHIONS TOGETHER If a cushion, for example, or a detail in a picture, is to be made really thick, the pieces should be folded or

A hole cut from the back to push filling in is sewn back together after the "operation"! Notice how the elephant becomes smaller and the material around it puckers. Allow for the filling with a little extra material.

Top and bottom view of small cushions filled and sewn together.

A cap may well need a padded, quilted edge. In this case both the crown and the edge are pleated.

gathered round the filling. The underside can be covered with smaller pieces and the edges joined together so that the cushions fit closely together, and look like well-risen buns that have run together. Using patches made from a knitted fabric gives a softer and rounder shape.

CLOTHES AND ACCESSORIES

Some of the techniques that have been described can be used when making clothes, handbags and so on. Sometimes filling is only required at certain points. If the material for a dress is thin, it may be a good idea to quilt the bodice and perhaps the lower part of the skirt. Shoulder straps and edges can also be padded. Choose a suitable filling material: a tie should have a thin

Both sides of a little cloth handbag. The central oval happened to fit into the flowery pattern of the material.

44

A much-used handbag of scraps of leather and flower-patterned cretonne. The filling of plastic foam has kept it springy and has helped to preserve the shape of the relief. Quilted with buttonhole silk, sewn by machine around the out-lines of the flower pattern.

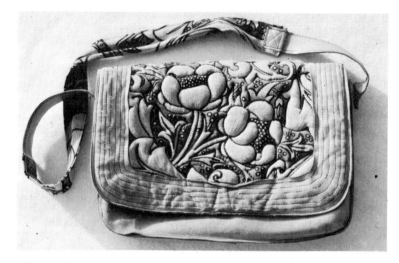

(flannel) lining and a handbag needs thick padding such as thin foam rubber. It is very practical to use the pattern on the material as the basis of your design. You can even use patterned backing material so that you don't need to draw on a pattern for quilting. For an example of a pattern sewn in this way, see the spiral pattern on p. 38.

BATIK DYEING AND HAND-PRINTING often produce patterns suitable for quilting. The cloth shown below was tacked and then dyed to produce an even, linear pattern, which is easy to follow when quilting on to a terry-towelling backing, and which is accentuated by the machine-stitching in a dark thread. Even the bottom thread is dark, to avoid small, light-coloured stitches being visible on the top fabric, which may occur if the thread tension on the machine is wrongly adjusted.

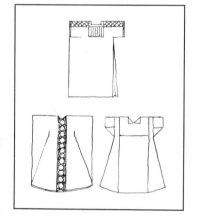

Suggestions for long or short straight styles with quilted sections. The width can be reduced by box pleats or seams, and the excess material either left in place or cut off. Gussets may be needed under the sleeves.

Batik-patterned cloth on white terry-towelling.

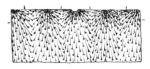

Bird-like in both design and material. A thin, hand-printed cotton with quilted sections at the neck and the elbows.

STRAIGHT LENGTHS It is pleasing to cut a beautiful piece of material as little as possible and still make a practical and comfortable garment, which permits great freedom of movement and suits everyone, especially the disabled. If you tire of a particular design, all you have to do is to unpick the seams and use the length of material in another way, perhaps even as a quilt. It is also possible to do the opposite – make clothes out of blankets, tablecloths or curtains. Appliqué work in thin material is suitable for blankets, and a curtain becomes more stable and less transparent with a porous backing or filling. A beautifully quilted section can be transferred from one garment to another.

The sides sewn together at the wrists. Padded edging at the neck.

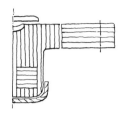

*Straight pieces, slits roun-
ded off. Bias-cut strips of
edging follow the shape
and overlap at the slits. The
jacket is reversible and has
double pockets and cuffs.
Strong handwoven cloth.*

*Straight quilted pieces can
be buttoned together by
means of squares like those
shown below, either let in
or sewn on.*

COATS AND JACKETS can be made from ready-quilted
fabric bought by the metre, or you can cut out the
material with the necessary seam allowances and quilt
it yourself. Choose good-quality material of a type that
is easy to work with, and pin and tack before quilting.

*Below, small duffle-coat with material from a blouse made
into a quilted lining. There was not enough material for any
overlap at the front, but it still made a warm, windproof coat,
thanks to the buttonhole loops as shown in the drawings. If
the material is thin it can be folded double with cord inside the
outer edge. In either case the edges folded over are stitched
down along the buttonhole stitching. Can also be made
square.*

with cord

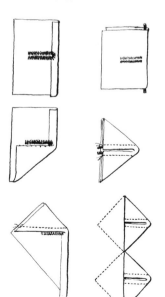

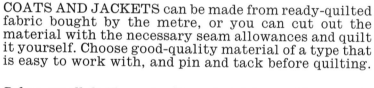

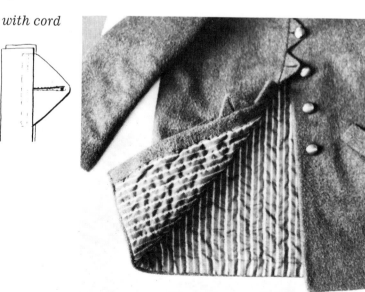

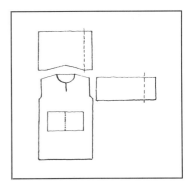

Long, reversible jacket with the stripes in different directions. Quilted as on p. 15. Edging strips of the same material with filling inside. Pockets optional.

Check that there are no creases on the backing. Striped material is easy to quilt, either backwards and forwards or in one direction only. If both sides are striped, lay them with the lengthwise grain of each at right-angles to the other, so that the stitching on the backing runs at right-angles to the stripes. There are various ways of joining the pieces together – for example, with binding covering the seams. To make a jacket or a coat warmer or more attractive, you can quilt a pretty lining for it.

When the child's waistcoat below was quilted the material pulled out of shape, resulting in even, diagonal wrinkles, which are not unattractive and make the waistcoat warmer. The same thing happened with the lining of the duffle-coat on p. 47.

QUILTED WAISTCOATS are very attractive garments. They are easy to sew in either cloth or leather, and can be made reversible if required. Choose the design and sewing method according to the materials you have on hand. The waistcoat below owes its unusual cut to the fact that the strips which were sewn together were too short. The waistcoat above was made from a tablecloth with a dotted pattern and a plain border. Stains were concealed under embroidery. The facing shrank so that the quilted lining became fuller and warmer. The filling of the violet child's waistcoat on the opposite page is an old woolly cardigan.

An embroidered Greek waistcoat of an unusual cut inspired the waistcoat above. It is made out of strips of corduroy from a pair of jeans and flower-patterned scraps of a material of the same weight, sewn together by machine using the technique shown on p. 32. Synthetic batting can with care be split into two layers; in this instance one such layer gave quite enough fulness and warmth. The plain lining is turned up around the edges – in some of the corners insets were needed – and the facing, filling and lining were joined together using feather-stitch.

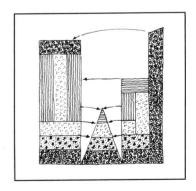

The gussets inserted in the embroidered waistcoat on the left could have been made from patches as shown in the diagram.

SLIP ON, TIE ON Waistcoats, a poncho and a heart-shaped "comforter" are shown here as examples of simple garments in snug materials. The poncho can be made of real or synthetic fur; the waistcoat of pieces of woollen cloth in a range of discreet colours, or of pieces of fur. The man's waistcoat, which had previously been a removable coat lining, is quilted along the lower edge to hold the woollen material and the lining together. This kind of edge is also useful on the front of a garment to keep the cloth out of the way of the zip. Along the bottom edge it prevents the lining from sagging.

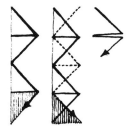

The quilted edge is stitched in two stages with the help of a triangular template which is moved along. Instead of stopping and starting, stitch forward and then back again across the middle of the square.

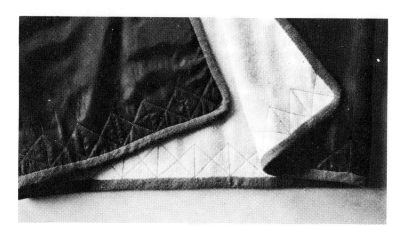

Apron made of patches attached to backing. Some of them can be pockets.

Reversible poncho in fur and imitation suede, held together with intertwined tendrils in chain-stitch.

Heart-shaped woollen "comforter", edged with binding, which could be worn, for example, underneath a coat in a cold car. Two pieces of an old sweater turned wrong side out, with small rings of buttonhole-stitch holding them together.

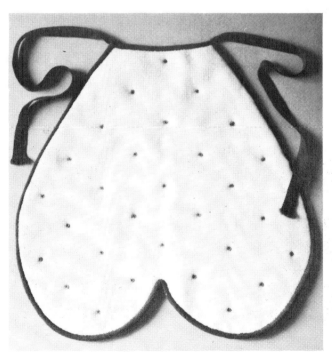

Bed rug to put on the floor, or to rest one's feet on when lying on the bed. Quilted nylon lining material with the edges sewn down beneath a material with a rougher surface. The square pattern is in stem-stitch running right through the rug.

PRE-QUILTED MATERIAL sold by the metre, or an old quilted garment, can also be used. There may be material on one or both sides of the filling. The example shown here has nylon material on one side. the travelling or sleeping bag is lined with a knitted cotton material. The bed rug shows how a basic square pattern can be used when quilting through an additional layer of material.

Thin ready-quilted nylon lining material and jersey, so pliable that it is possible to sew pleats to let out when the baby gets bigger. Press-fasteners are better than a zip in such soft material, and won't break either.

The cape above is made from ready-quilted cotton material edged with binding, and consists of a square with sewn pleats and an opening for the head. The child's cape below in almost luminous orange nylon is meant to be buttoned into place below the collar of a child's overall. It can be made in a variety of designs as protection from the rain and to make a child more easily seen. It is an excellent plan to stitch on reflective tabs or material. When cutting out quilted material it is important to secure the cut ends of the quilting threads in some way, such as by machine stitching around the edges.

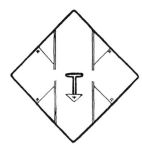

Pleats sewn on the inside and the outside make the material fold the way intended. Press-fasteners hold the sleeves together.

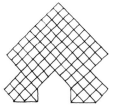

Child's cape made by following the edges of the squares of ready-made nylon quilting. Front corners fastened by Velcro tape or press-fasteners.

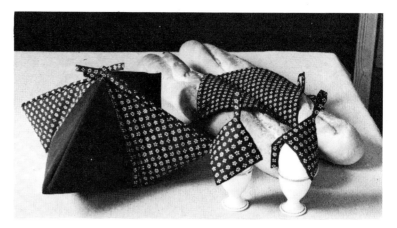

Egg cosies or loaf holders made from four squares all the same size, with filling. Two are sewn together diagonally and laid, together with filling, between the other two. Held together with small stitches or quilting, and edged.

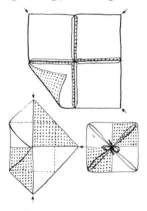

Small tablecloth which can be turned into a bundle. Four squares are sewn together, the corners folded in towards the centre and sewn together with the seams inwards. One is left open until the filling has been added. Quilting holds the layers together and marks where to fold it.

AROUND THE HOUSE

PROTECTION AGAINST BUMPS, HEAT, COLD AND DAMP   Using new or old material you can sew practical and unusual handbags, storage bags, and cases for fragile objects such as bottles, photographic equipment and instruments. A well-fitted-out and sufficiently strong home-made case is as good as a bought one, and people are less likely to suspect that the contents may be valuable. Bags for keeping things hot or cold are useful in the home as well as on outings. It is a good idea to try to make things that can be used in various ways and in different circumstances. This is also the way to approach your materials. A sleeve from a quilted jacket, for example, could become a cover for a bottle, a wrist, ankle or knee protector, or even a barbecue glove if made of non-inflammable material with sufficient insulation. If you unpick the seams of the sleeve, many other uses will become possible.

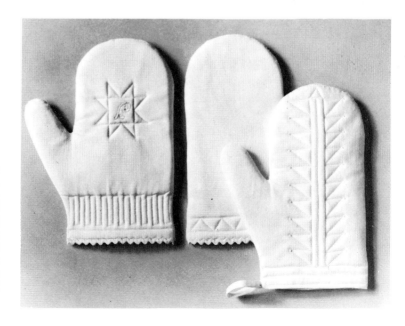

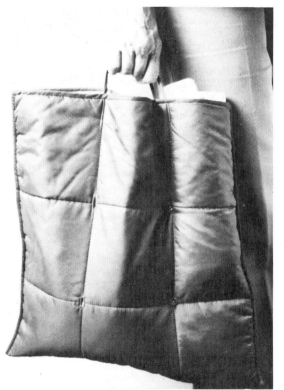

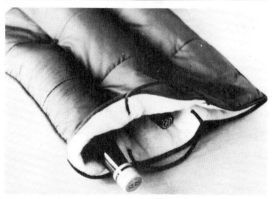

Bag with one, two or three compartments, which could be used, for example, as combined hand-luggage and cushion when travelling. There are buttons and buttonholes for dividing it up to separate fragile objects from each other.

You can avoid fitting a zip or sewing buttonholes in a bag by making it out of a blouse or jacket with these already fitted. The bag on the left is made from a blouse, and quilted with a plain lining and filled with plastic foam.

Quilted sleeve made into a bag for a vacuum flask.

Cushion for triangular chair-bottom.

Foldable cushion. Stars made by sewing together triangles or folded strips (see p. 83) in appliqué on terry-towelling. The edges are hemmed and two out of three joins are sewn together.

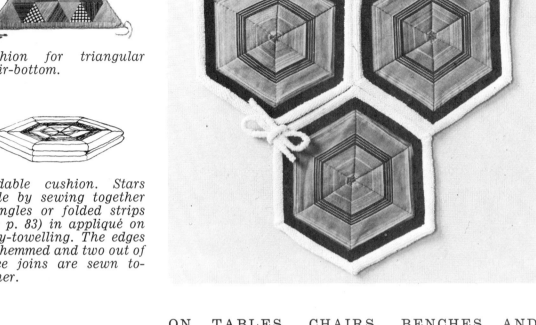

Bath mat in terry-towelling and chair bottom of hand-woven cloth and strips of cloth intended for rug-making. Both backed with foam rubber.

ON TABLES, CHAIRS, BENCHES AND FLOORS Tablecloths, table runners and mats protect the surface of a table. Cushions, whether fitted or loose, can be made not only for ordinary chairs but also for rocking chairs, wheelchairs and seats at work. A rather delicate large carpet or a fitted carpet needs protection at heavily used places and a bathroom mat can have an anti-slip backing attached to it.

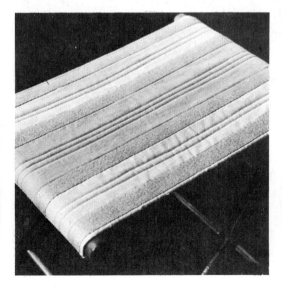

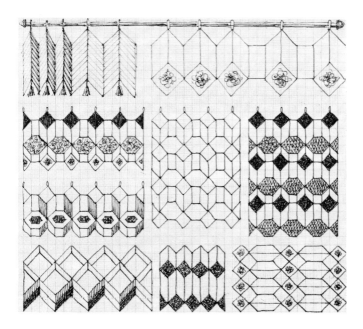

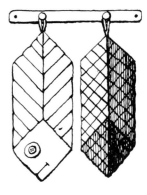

Pot-holder that looks like a fish – if sewn double it can be slipped over a hot handle, e.g. a barbecue skewer. Fir-cones and flowers can be made in the same way. If joined together in rows they can form edges for quilts, tablecloths, curtain pelmets. Here scraps of material with jugendstil embroidery in pearl cotton have been made use of.

FOR DOORS AND WINDOWS A piece of quilting either to hang on the wall or use as a curtain not only looks warm and cosy, it also insulates against both cold and noise. Quilting is also suitable for folding screens. These often stand with their sections at angles so that the relief, with its variations of tone and shade, is seen to advantage. It is a good idea to allow the pleats of curtain pelmets, privacy screens and curtains to occur naturally at lines of quilting and seams. They will then fold easily together like an accordion. Quilting using transparent fabrics produces special effects, see pp. 50 and 108.

Cushion for a bench made from beautiful fabrics in shades of blue from Swaziland.

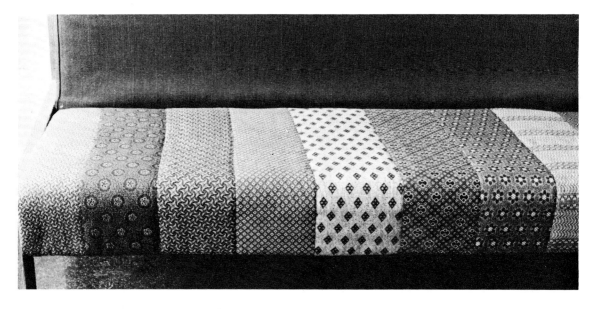

"Picture" and frame made from a single piece of cotton material with a large square pattern. The frame is formed by making a stitched pleat from the wrong side around the edge, which is thus lifted up. Strips of filling are then put in place, the corners formed and stitched at the same time as the edges are folded back and sewn down. In the centre, an appliqué patch of silk with elephants.

Right, experimenting with squared paper to create patterns. If the seams are marked in, the finished product looks like a leaded window.

MATERIALS WITH LARGE SQUARES OR CHECKS can, by means of quilting, be used to produce a variety of patterns for quilts, mats, cushions, protective wall-hangings, tablecloths, handbags etc. Choose a filling of the appropriate thickness, and let the quilting follow the pattern in one way or another. The squares can become rooms, backyards, houses, seen from the side or from above. Allow your imagination to play with such ideas as terraces of houses, tower blocks with balconies and awnings, even perhaps swimming pools. In the absence of suitable material with a pattern of large squares, you can sew large patches together.

When travelling one often sees views of houses and villages which form beautiful patterns. A quick sketch in a notebook became a quilted square with black machine-stitching on a white background. The houses could also be sewn on square-patterned, bleached or unbleached hand-woven linen, as a regular repetitive pattern or as a free composition.

A common method to avoid having to secure the ends of threads is to sew forwards and then backwards along the same line.

Sketches and experimental pieces – quilting on square-patterned material.

Three patches stitched together and a well-padded frame look like a cell with bars.

PICTURES OF INDOOR AND OUTDOOR SCENES can easily be made by using the techniques described on pp. 32 and 33. These may simply be pictures, or even "wall-theatres".

Like a cinema, with rows of people and interchangeable "screen" squares.

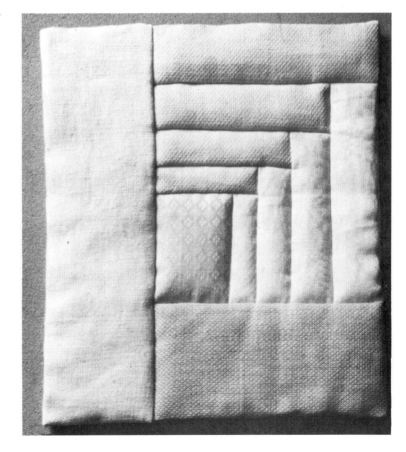

Like an ancient temple – column after column, or white marble walls – sewn out of strips of hand-woven tablecloth material.

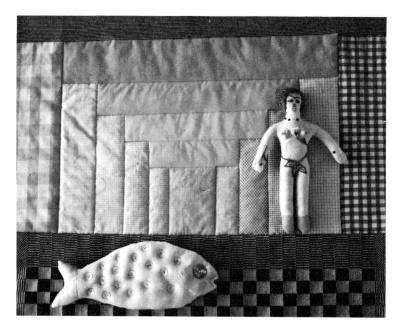

A stage that can be turned around and altered. Here it looks like a swimming pool with a chequered bottom and a goldfish, seen from low down.

Here it is seen from a higher level, and shows different scenes with dolls as the actors, and a gingham curtain. It could also be a street or market scene.

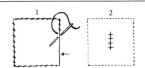

1. Attach the patch by hand using e.g. concealed stitching or blanket stitch. Push the filling in before the last few stitches are made.

2. Sew the patch on, push the filling in through a hole in the underside and then repair the hole.

3. Lay the filling on the underside of the patch, fold down and secure the edges, turn the patch over and sew into place.

4. Lay the filling under the patch, sew with close or open zig-zag stitching and trim off any material left outside as seam allowance.

APPLIQUÉ WORK

PADDED APPLIQUÉ WORK can be simple and yet very elegant, depending on the quality of the material, the colours and the workmanship. The soft woollen cushion is decorated with a small padded square of silk on a large padded square of poplin. On page 68 the same square is shown extended by the addition of triangles. There are many ways of attaching padded patches. The drawings show four different techniques, and of course the patches can be of irregular shape, such as those in the drawing on p. 41.

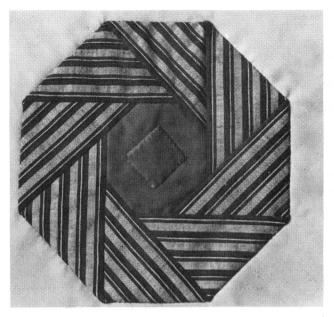

PERSPECTIVE The hexagon which looks like a cube can be endlessly used, varied and repeated, for instance as a patch to mend a hole. It is easy and enjoyable to devise patterns using squared paper, such as large perspective designs for appliqué-work wall-hangings or patchwork. Mix patchwork and appliqué work. An appliqué-work patch can be made up of smaller patches joined together.

Block for a quilt, or a pot-holder.

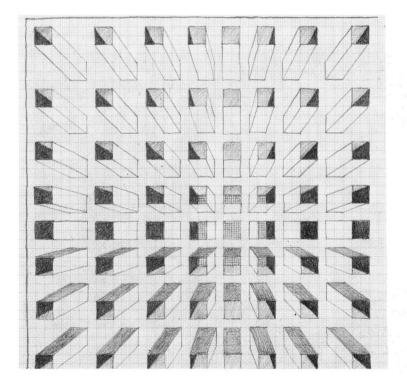

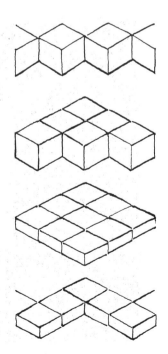

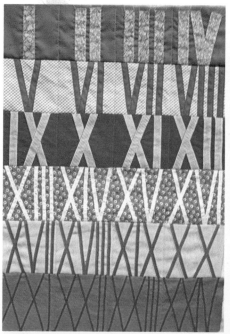

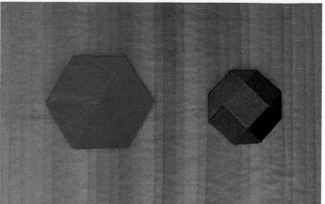

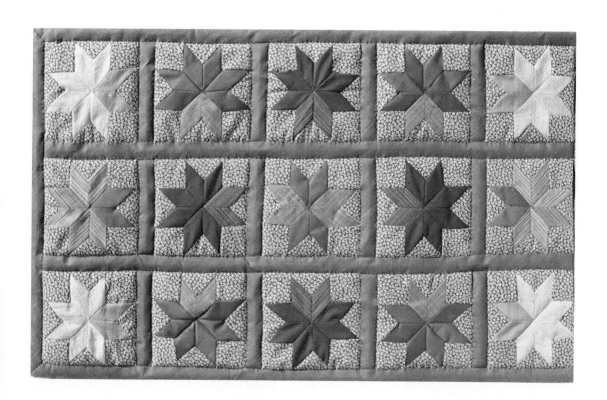

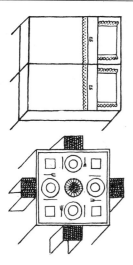

Above and on page 74, table and chairs according to the same principle. Can be placed straight or diagonally.

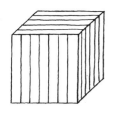

If you use two striped materials, or different widths between the lines of quilting, the illusion of depth becomes more convincing than simply using outlines.

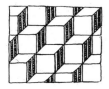

SIMPLIFIED PERSPECTIVE, sometimes called oblique parallel projection, is suitable for both patchwork and appliqué work. It may be used for designs with motifs such as houses, rooms, furniture and so on. Cut out rectangular patches which may, for example, represent beds seen from above, and place them either obliquely as in the photograph, or straight as in the drawing and add headboards and legs. On the next page are shown a table and chairs represented in the same simple way. The illustrations also show how to make use of fabric samples, lace and embroidered fabrics.

The twill mat shown above is intended as a plaything for both children and parents. It represents a room furnished with padded beds sewn in place, which can be used either as dolls' beds or children's pillows. Other pieces of furniture may be made in the same way. The mat can also be used as a wall-hanging with movable dolls.

The drawing of a cube shows a slightly different method. The front is a square and the receding lines are at angles of 45°, or half a right-angle. This method is an easy way of

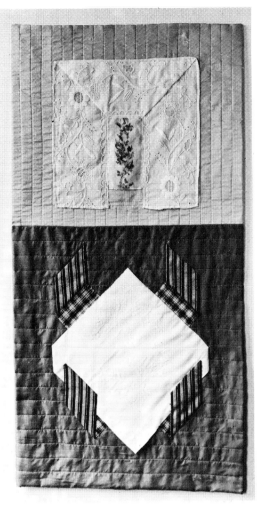

Vertical quilting as a wall and horizontal as a floor. Window with flowers and lace curtains. Table with white cloth and chairs round it. Intended as a wall-hanging and to make use of delicate embroidery and ribbon.

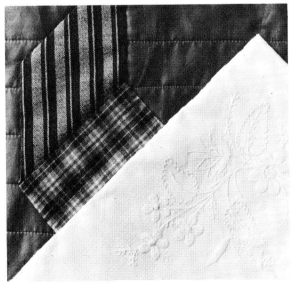

forming patterns to cover whole surfaces, either in patchwork or appliqué work or just quilting. Some of the patches may also be decorated with embroidery.

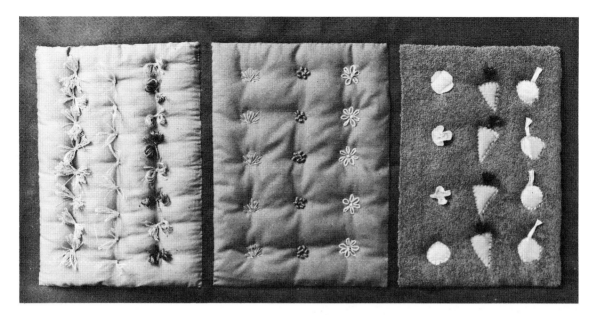

Three padded patches used to try out various materials and ways of sewing. Thin material with knotted thread ends, poplin with small embroidered motifs and stretch terry-towelling with patches sewn on by hand.

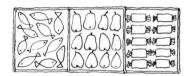

Fish, fruit and toffees.

CUT-OUT PATCHES used in appliqué work are best sewn in place with stitching that runs right through the work so that it is quilted at the same time. The stitches need not be visible if the edges of the material are folded under. If the stitching has to cover a ragged edge, use zig-zag machine stitching, blanket stitch, feather-stitch, herringbone-stitch or a similar type of stitch. Large areas between patches can be quilted in simple patterns and large patches quilted in various ways, such as by means of threads pulled through and knotted, by embroidery or appliqué work or by quilted patterns. The test piece above looks like garden plots or hot-beds. A good exercise in using knotting, embroidery and appliqué work might be to illustrate a garden or a vegetable stall.

Small round shapes like lettuces; carrots; and onions with short stems.

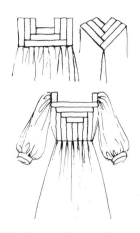

Quilted patch on the front of a bodice can be sewn either flat or shaped, using the log-cabin technique.

MENDING, PATCHING AND ADAPTING

MAKE CLOTHES MORE DISTINCTIVE OR MORE USEFUL A ready-to-wear garment can be made more attractive, larger, smaller, warmer or stronger by means of quilting, whether it is a tailored or a knitted garment. If the material is elastic, get someone else to try it on, or at least check what it looks like when worn, before you sew any patches or insets into place. Otherwise you may find that the result is too tight-fitting and pulls unattractively at the material. It may be a good idea to make belts, handbags and hats in material which matches the applied-work motifs.

Two pot-holders changed a soft, warm, knitted skirt into a top, comfortable when worn over a blouse and wide enough for a maternity garment.

Two bags made from material left over from the dress on the right. One was sewn to try letting the unpressed seams stand up on the reverse and fitting the filling between these ridges. The other is opened by means of pressure on the ends of the padded edges, which are stiffened by means of flexible strips cut from a plastic lid.

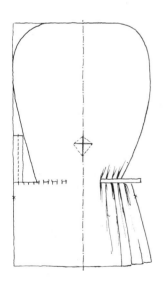

Strip of cloth cut into pointed shapes, padded and sewn on around a padded neck opening. The dress is a simple design using a single piece of cloth.

SEW PATCHES on elbows, knees and the seats of trousers, even if they are not worn out. A padded patch protects against wear and feels warm and soft. Sufferers from rheumatism with sore joints that need protection from bumps will benefit particularly from patches with a suitable filling, either detachable or sewn in place.

Plastic or foam rubber padding provides the best protection against damp. Sew it in place at the same time as you sew on the patch, either by quilting or with stitches at intervals from the underside. Sometimes it is difficult to sew patches on without unpicking a seam. It is always possible by hand, but machine stitching is both quicker and stronger. Sports clothes need thickly padded areas as protection at exposed or vulnerable places. Good sports clothes for children can be made from strong jersey fabric in bright colours, although for older children stronger fabrics are better.

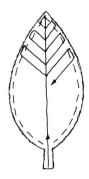

Tack the leaf in place, sew first along the central vein, then back and forth and finally zig-zag around the edge, either close or open.

An appliqué-work snake which coils round the bottom and the knees, and large "sticking-plaster" patches – if crazy ideas appeal to you, the possibilities are endless.

An eye-catching design on a pocket. In this case the seat of a pair of corduroy jeans has been made into a bag to thread on to a belt made out of the waistband of the same jeans.

DECORATIVE PATCHES such as monograms, symbols and badges can also be padded. Round shapes look most effective in relief.

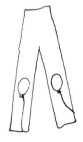

Real balloons burst if you crawl on them. Perhaps these will help to discourage crawling.

CONVEX SHAPES are very suitable for handbags, elbow protectors and so on, or as a way of emphasizing the roundness of a flower, for example. One way of making such convex rounded shapes is to quilt outwards from a large or small central round shape. The patch can be quilted before being sewn in place on the material.

Experiments with different materials. Top left, padded flower sewn on to a knitted background. Bottom, both sides of a circle cut to make a neck opening, before it was sewn on to a plain backing to make a round handbag.

Remove a triangle from a hexagon to make a convex pentagon. Lower down, round designs which can be sewn on a machine without breaks in the stitching.

Make use of materials to hand. Above, a square of shot silk quilted and sewn on to a silk handkerchief. Right, a cushion with a flower made from an un-picked bow-tie similar to that shown below.

Below, a strip suitable for a lampshade or a dress, made of thin material sewn on to thin synthetic batting.

APPLIQUÉ WORK IN SEVERAL LAYERS This
appliqué-work waistcoat from Norway has symmetrical
motifs arranged symmetrically. Blanket-stitch, stem-
stitch and chain-stitch are used to attach the patches
and to increase the relief effect, and the background is
decorated with small stitches. The whole effect is the
result of a combination of form, colour and the struc-
tures of the materials and the embroidery.

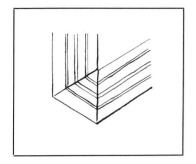

The hexagonal shape here is folded out of a strip of striped material rather than sewn together out of triangles. It is easy to use the folds to obtain a slightly convex shape.

THIN CLOTH ON FELT An old beret or hat can be rejuvenated by means of appliqué-work patches. The material used may perhaps match that of a blouse or scarf. Padding is not necessary; since the felt is fairly springy, it gives the quilting some relief and the appliqué patch makes the hat warmer. Pieces of a beret or a hat make an ideal filling for warm, soft, quilted areas at elbows, knees and shoulders, for example for people who suffer from rheumatism. It is also useful as a material for appliqué work, since it will not fray.

The hat on the right and a detail from the waistcoat on the left are shown in colour on p. 70.

THIN CLOTH ON KNITTED FABRICS makes such garments more wind-proof, and also helps to prevent rolling. Stitch the material to a well-stretched backing and it will subsequently become slightly elastic and "bubbly". Use like quilting.

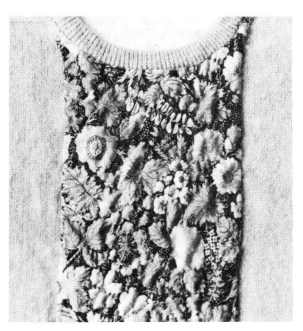

You can make mittens on a sewing machine out of two knitted sleeves or the legs of socks. They become warmer and more attractive with the addition of appliqué patches, quilted on to them.

THIN CLOTH ON CROCHETED FABRICS If you are bored with an old hat you can liven it up by adding ribbon and strips of flower-patterned material. The ribbon in the illustration is quilted along its centre, and the material is quilted between the flowers, see p. 9.

If you have spent a lot of time quilting a garment and then grown tired of it, pieces of the quilting can be cut out and re-used.

85

A piece of curtain material with scraps of embroidered material sewn on can be dyed and used as a head-scarf or shawl. This one, reputedly from Denmark, is in a beautiful blue-grey.

USE HEADSQUARES AND HANDKERCHIEFS for appliqué work and patchwork. If the material is thin or worn, quilting is particularly suitable.

A small motif, sewn in between the layers of a very thin headscarf folded double, or in appliqué work, decorates and also stops it flapping in the wind.

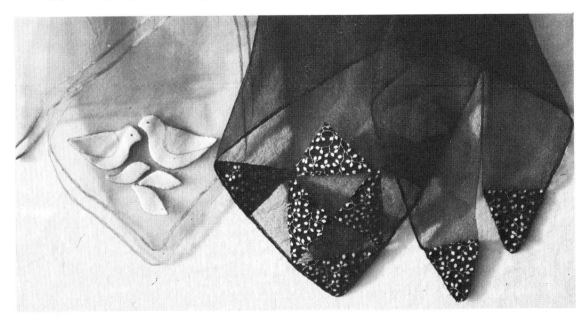

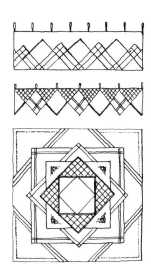

Handkerchiefs of varying quality and striped, chequered or patterned are suitable for appliqué work. With a transparent filling they are suitable for curtain pelmets, lampshades etc. Can also be used for edging, babies' quilts, tablecloths, or perhaps decorations on blouses. For a tablecloth, such as that shown in the drawing, single handkerchiefs can be used near the centre, and further out handkerchiefs of which there are at least two. For the smaller corners each handkerchief is cut into four parts, for the larger corners, diagonally into two.

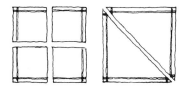

Appliqué-work corner on a silk scarf.

RAGS TORN INTO STRIPS FOR RUG-MAKING can be used for the items illustrated here – as insets in a dress, decorations on a skirt and jumper, and sewn together to make a dress, a silk tablecloth and a handbag.

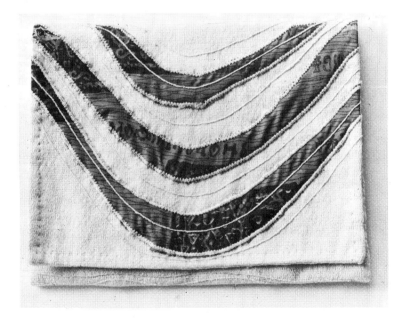

The two sides of a handbag – strips attached by means of zig-zag stitching over coarse thread.

The dark strips on the bag on the left, judging by their shape, were cut from a sleeve. The strips on the skirt and the tablecloth were so pliant that they could be cut straight but sewn on in wavy lines. Decorative machine stitching.

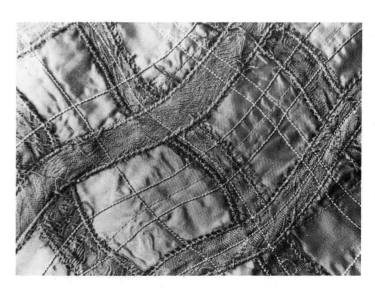

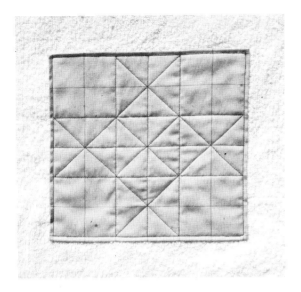

GAMES like ludo, fox and geese, and chess can be used as decorative devices that can actually be used, on cushions, rugs and bath-towels. If terry-towelling is used no filling is necessary. If it shrinks the patches will become a little more "bubbly", but it is important that the patches do not shrink. The cushion cover below is not a game but an experimental design produced by cutting crosses in checked material and turning under and stitching down the edges to reveal the pattern of the material below.

Useful motifs – both for appliqué and quilting – for those who enjoy card games.

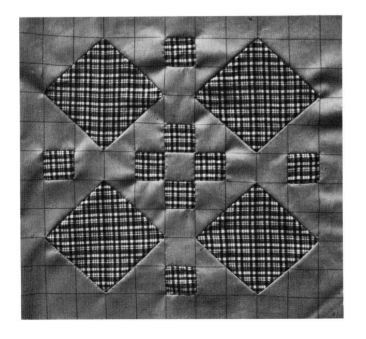

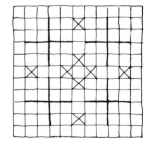

The edges are easier to handle if the points are left on after the crosses have been cut.

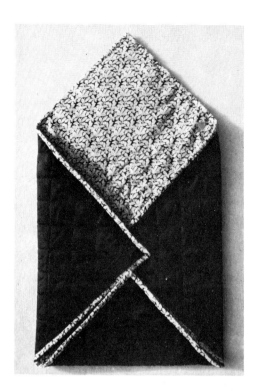

Appliqué on background quilted in squares – both ornament and chess board. Stones, pine cones or seed cases can be used as pieces. Can also be used as cushion to sit on or put the feet up on when travelling. Easy to fold into a bag.

Dice are decorative forms to quilt with appliqué-work patches or with buttons, or used as hexagons in patchwork mosaic or appliqué. Can also be used as an idea for a case or a cushion.

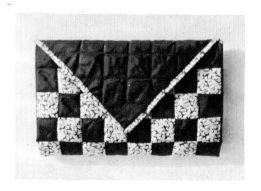

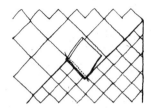

On white material quilted in squares, the patches along the edges can form hearts.

Suggested method for sewing the patches on one by one either by machine or using running-stitch. Note that the left-hand edge is folded so that it can be sewn on to the previous row. If the backing had been quilted in larger squares the resulting quilt would have been thicker.

A MOSAIC OF PATCHES ON QUILTED MATERIAL is a much easier job than joining the patches together first and quilting afterwards. The patches can either be sewn on to the back of the filling, in which case they should cover the entire surface, or they can be sewn at intervals to the facing – see the bag on the previous page. Large and small patches can be used. They can cover one or more of the quilted squares, according to the pattern used, and may either be sewn on by hand with the edges turned under or mainly by machine like the child's quilt above.

The large leaves on this quilt are mixed with the unobtrusive finely patterned pieces giving a pleasing effect. If it were not for these, the coverlet could have been quilted right across the squares along the lines of quilting which can be seen as faint shadowy markings below. A quilt with a toothed edge on all the sides that hang down looks attractive on a bed.

Pot-holder with the letter S in patchwork or appliqué.

Appliqué-work patches such as those in the top picture must be of the correct size and density to suit the backing material.

USE THE SHEEN OF THE MATERIAL Place pieces of shot material with the grain at different angles. The unfinished piece of work above, of silk with different warps and wefts, is intended as a decorative panel for a dress. It could also be made into a handbag. The black and white backing material (top) has low, round, padded pieces of velour in shades of red. These take on different sheens according to the direction of the grain. More examples may be seen on pp. 14 and 49.

On the right a wall hanging of quilted, striped curtain material. The lining carries on round the edges on the short sides. On the long sides are taut strips of material. The rather flat appliqué-work decorations appear raised because pale, shiny pieces are turned in one direction and dark, matt ones in another. For the full effect the wall-hanging should be placed so that the lighting enhances this illusion.

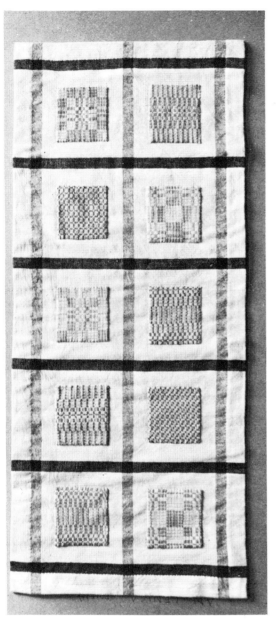

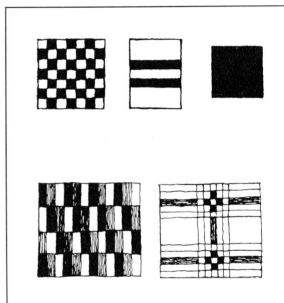

SCRAPS OF HAND-WOVEN MATERIAL are worth making use of both as backing and as appliqué-work patches. If you make a sampler from pieces of hand-woven cloth made, for example, by members of the family, you will also find that your interest in weaving techniques is stimulated. Pieces from worn-out table runners, both right and wrong sides uppermost, were used to make the tablecloth above. There is flannel under the square-patterned background material, and the patches and the hems are sewn with stitches that run right through.

Striped, chequered and plain materials can be sewn together to form patterns which look like hand-woven material, like the tablecloth above. Woven patterns can also be enlarged and sewn by joining together plain patches and binding as shown in the drawing.

A soft, light, hand-woven blanket was mended and used as a filling. It is easy to lay out the patches and sew them into place and add the lining afterwards.

A blanket with round patches sewn on at the same time as the lining, and given a new lease of life either as a quilt or a curtain.

The same square-patterned blanket as that shown on p. 69, but here with patches over different rectangles. Blankets are ideal as a combined filling and backing. The patches can also be quilted.

OLD PIECES OF EMBROIDERED MATERIALS, LACE
AND SAMPLES of various kinds of cloth can be taken
out of store and used to make pictures that will give
great pleasure.

*Detail of the wall-hanging
shown on p. 11.*

*An embroidered heart, im-
proved by quilting.*

A piece of worn hand-woven material, lined with white flannel, with rows of chain-stitch in linen thread.

A piece left over and used as appliqué work on linen to make a handbag to match. Edging strip from the same material.

LEARNING FROM PRIMITIVE PEOPLES

Primitive peoples such as the Amerindians can teach us a great deal about patterns, techniques and ways of using fabrics. They make straight lengths of cloth and sew them together into practical and beautiful clothes without cutting any more than necessary. Their methods of hemming, joining and sewing together are very decorative. Their simple and practical necklines are often made by means of straight cuts with the edges and points folded in or out, or sometimes by cutting out an oval hole. These can be very useful techniques.

CUTTING STRAIGHT OR CURVED LINES AND FOLDING THEM IN   The work illustrated on pages 99 and 116 is from Laos, and was made by cutting in spirals, in circles and in right-angles through a layer of facing material, and folding in and stitching the edges down on to the layer of material below, as in the *mola* technique. The stitches also run through a lining. The technique is mixed with conventional appliqué work and

Above and right, the simplest neck-hole imaginable – a slit between two selvedges. Above, examples of edging and joining techniques from Guatemala.

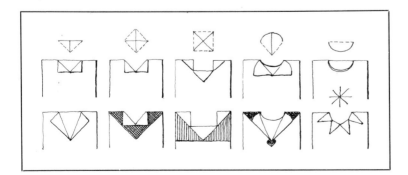

Simple cut-out neck holes. No material is cut away, the points are folded out and stitched down, with filling if required. Three of these suggestions have yokes sewn on.

embroidery, all very finely and skilfully done. The work from Laos provided the inspiration for the baby's quilt below, although it is decorated with appliqué work, using bias binding folded double and raised by sewing with the needle in a zig-zag below the binding and through the top fabric, the filling and the backing. Sewing the binding on by the machine would of course be much quicker, but the result would not be comparable.

STRIP AFTER STRIP, WITH FOLDS AT THE CORNERS The heart-shaped decoration from Thailand (p. 100) shows the result of sewing narrow strips of fabric in different colours on to a backing one after another, starting from a patch in the centre. The

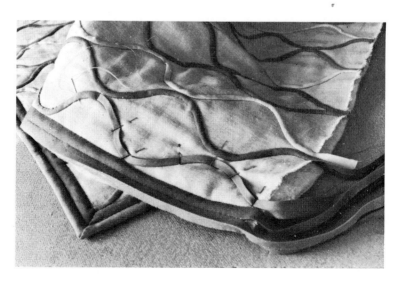

Drawing of the top and underside shows how the strips of double-folded bias binding are sewn on. The edging strips are simple, the outer one is taken round the edge and sewn on to the lining.

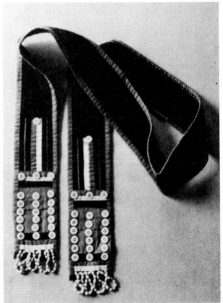

stitching, which runs right through several layers of cloth, fastens the folded edge of each strip down over the rough edge of the previous strip. The strips are folded at each corner, and in the centre there is additional appliqué work.

Belt from Thailand. Band sewn in place with small running stitches in silk. Buttons and seeds threaded like beads add weight and decoration.

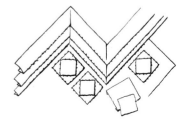

The heart above left inspired the tea-cosy which was made as shown by the drawing below.

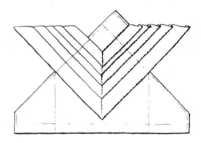

Front of a blouse in the mola technique with appliqué-work patches and embroidery.

Examples of the way in which the Indians vary their techniques, cutting black and red cloth at the same time, removing one or other material alternately so that the pieces resemble a jig-saw puzzle. The edges are folded down and sewn on to white cloth.

HOLES WITHIN HOLES THROUGH SEVERAL LAYERS OF CLOTH The Cuna Indians adapted designs originally used for body-painting for use in appliqué work on blouses called *molas*. In *mola* work the fine detail of the pattern is typically achieved by cutting progressively smaller holes in each layer of material, so that they all become visible. The edges are folded under and secured by stitches running right through all the layers. This technique is also called reverse appliqué work. A variation is to insert pieces of cloth in different colours through the holes – see the bird in the colour picture on p. 114. The patterns consist of abstract shapes, symbols, plants, animals and motifs drawn from everyday life. See p. 115 for an experimental design using striped material.

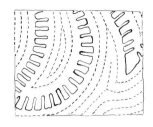

Quilt from Pennsylvania with "Prince of Wales' feathers". The symmetrical details and the wavy lines of quilting are reminiscent of Hawaii; the cut-out shapes and edges folded in resemble the mola *technique.*

FOLDING AND CUTTING is a common way of making patterns. Hawaii, for example, has a special type of appliqué work, in which large patterns with plant motifs are worked outwards from the centre, the diagonals or the edge of a quilt. The patterns are cut out by using folded paper – see p. 21. The edges of the material are folded under as the work progresses, using the point of the sewing needle. The quilting follows the outlines of the patterns.

Techniques and materials were brought to Hawaii by missionaries. The patterns and sewing techniques developed on the islands then spread back to the mainland. They are now used in many variations like that on the left. Below, a positive-negative design made from felted wool folded and then cut, and stitched together edge to edge.

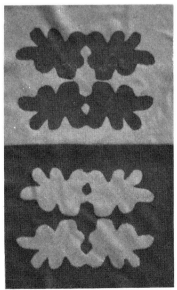

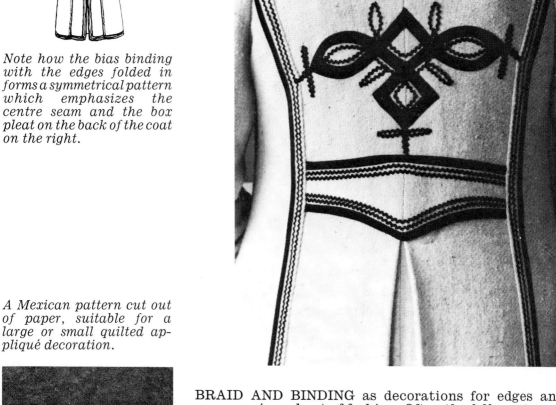

Note how the bias binding with the edges folded in forms a symmetrical pattern which emphasizes the centre seam and the box pleat on the back of the coat on the right.

A Mexican pattern cut out of paper, suitable for a large or small quilted appliqué decoration.

BRAID AND BINDING as decorations for edges and seams go in and out of fashion. Often the folk-costumes of various lands serve as models. Above, the pattern from an Amerindian costume has been adapted to decorate a coat in hand-woven white wool with black strips of cloth and binding. This is an example of the way in which traditional patterns are adapted in Guatemala to suit individual designs. Similar processes occur in Mediterranean lace-making. Every culture has a valuable inheritance to be treasured and developed.

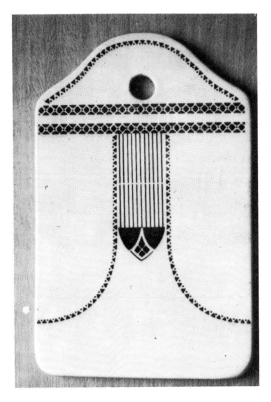

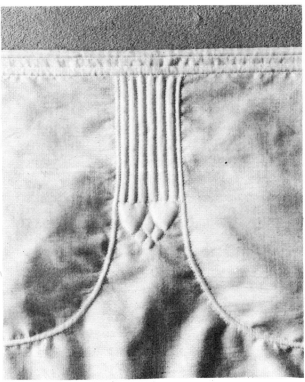

PATTERNS, PICTURES, IMAGINATION

Even if the text of this book is often concerned with techniques or use of materials, the illustrations are mainly of patterns. Examples of the taste and sense of form of primitive peoples, showing interplay of line, volume and colour, are illustrated on pp. 114–16. Pages 64–75 show certain techniques which can be used to create three-dimensional effects.

This section is mainly about images, ornaments, symbols and signs. Once one's eyes are alerted to such motifs, one sees almost everything around one translated into patterns for appliqué work and quilting – patterns on wallpaper, materials, embroidery and everyday objects.

The design on the chopping board above, for example, could be used in various ways; on hems, as a decoration round a neckline, on button-up plackets or pockets with reinforcement below, or at the waist of a skirt or apron.

Most exciting of all is to recreate designs straight from life. Examples of easy designs are the tracks in snow or sand on p. 18 and the plates with food on p. 106. The design of traffic on p. 124 and the houses with reflections in water on p. 4 are a little more complicated, but if

These blue decorations on a ceramic chopping-board are so suitable for appliqué work with patches and binding that one feels like trying something more original. The pattern immediately suggests line of quilting in blue, finished with three small or one large triangle.

Thin, double cotton cloth with thick wool pulled through between machine stitching. Padding in the same shade of white in the triangle. Could possibly be used on a blouse, a dress or a nightie, on the back and the front of the bodice and on the sleeves. Could also, for example, be used successfully in a jugendstil interior to create shadow effects on the curtains.

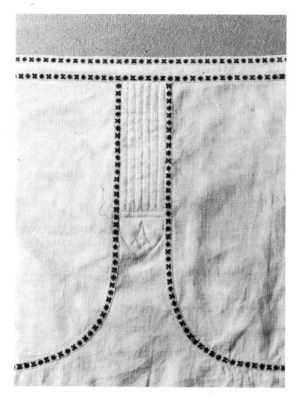

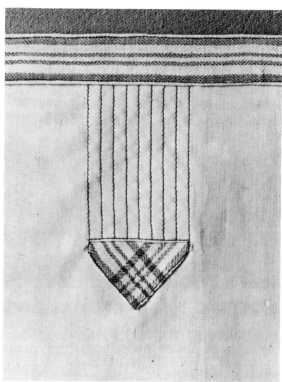

Here the quilting is sewn against a piece of flannel so that a white-on-white relief effect is produced. Old-fashioned braid in a curve suits the way a blouse is tailored at the waist or the edges of the pockets on an apron. The material is white linen. Might also provide ideas for a chair-back cushion.

Borders and corners from hand-woven towels have a lot of uses. Here a bias-cut strip is quilted in place below the facing and the actual corner protrudes through a slit in the material. An easy type of decoration to sew, which can be used in many ways; for instance, on tablecloths and aprons.

you choose to view the motif from either right above or straight in front it becomes quite easy. Motifs such as boxes of fish, fruit or vegetables, p. 75, the house with flower beds on p. 72 and the birds and fish on pp. 121, and 122 can be represented in the same way.

The examples in this book are very simple pictorial representations, but quilting is also very suitable for more complex pictures such as portraits, foreshortened figures, interiors and scenery in perspective. You can project sketches and transparencies of a suitable size on to paper and mark out the most important outlines.

With a little imagination the pictures can be made more or less three-dimensional, with interchangeable details, and they can be used, for example, as therapy for the partially sighted and other handicapped people.

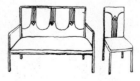

Fruit made of patches of material can be quilted to make table-mats and pot-holders, or even as table-decorations. The same is true of such ideas as plates of food, pieces of cheese, and round, flat loaves. Make them of patches of cloth, felt, backing material and edge with binding.

MOTIFS FROM EVERYDAY LIFE

PICTURES TO HANG ON THE WALL, perhaps to give as presents or souvenirs of home, might use such design motifs as the china and glass in the cupboard, the silver spoons in their box, or the food itself. Finely flower-patterned material can be used for cups or jugs, and a bowl or soup tureen can be quilted in soft white material. Leaf through your cookery book and have another look in the rag drawer. You may suddenly get an idea for a new type of wall-hanging or table decoration. It would, for example, be easy to sew a design of various kinds of pastries on a baking sheet, or of waffles, biscuits and wafers.

Globe artichoke made of pieces of linen. Shaped and padded leaves, against a background which gives a sense of space because of the different widths and light tones of the joined strips. (See p. 120.)

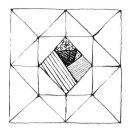

The frieze at the top of a tiled stove provided the idea for a square using the log-cabin technique, and the moulding and the decorated corner on the ceiling the inspiration for a white-on-white quilted design.

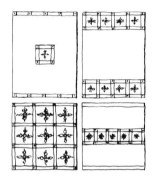

Left, drawings showing how squares can be arranged on quilts and tablecloths.

DIFFERENT STYLES can be copied from museums or from books, including not only the styles of other periods but also decorations from other countries. Often there is ornamentation all around us, both inside and on the outsides of houses. Taking the *jugendstil* ornament on the blanket shown below, two squares were made, which could be used for upholstery or quilts, bags, etc. That on the right was sewn together from pieces with close zig-zag stitching over the seams and round the apples and leaves. The leaf patterns in the corners are in zig-zag stitching alone, as are the main outlines of the square with round appliqué-work shapes on p. 108. This was made from a guest-towel with a square pattern, with a filling and a backing which give relief and stability. It could, for example, be made into a handbag.

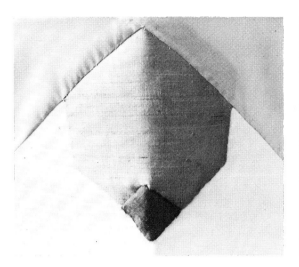
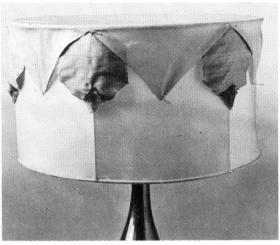

LEADED WINDOW EFFECTS If you choose silk as
both backing and top fabric and use thin synthetic
batting, you can make lampshades, screens, curtain
pelmets and window ornaments with a translucent
effect. Pad the whole piece of work and stitch shapes and
appliqué work with close zig-zag stitching, or pad and
attach motifs on to thin, taut fabric. For lampshades,
choose a pattern that fits in with the positions of the
wires of the frame. Experiment to see what it will look
like when the light shines through before you sew the
patches on. The wall-hanging below is made of nine
padded squares sewn together with small squares over
the corners. It is shown in colour on p. 69; patchwork
with light shining through it like a stained-glass
window, p. 50; a geometrical, rectilinear, recurring
pattern on p. 62.

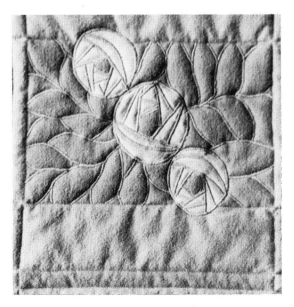

The frog was cut out with ample seam allowance, as was the filling. The edges were trimmed off after the zig-zag stitching was done. The edges of the flower are folded under and sewn with concealed stitching, and the inner shapes with small running stitches. The filling and backing are continuous and the stitching runs right through.

SOFT ROUND SHAPES are suitable for both appliqué-work and quilting – for example, natural shapes such as plants, fruit, shells and animals. Cut them out of patterned material or copy pictures from such sources as old engravings, school wall-charts and photographs. Pressed flowers and leaves can be traced from life or enlarged. The leaf on page 111 was traced from a living leaf. A quilt made of squares in shades of green with the outlines of large leaves quilted one to a square would look fresh and inviting. The illustration below showing eggs,

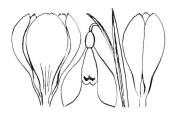

These design motifs from the plates in an old botanical work can be seen as appliqué work in colour on the cover.

Below, detail from the colour illustration. Right, one of the fruits in yellow satin, the other in moss-green corduroy. Organza seen from the side has the right sort of sheen for leaves and fruit. Red zig-zag round stones of wrinkled lining material, background of unbleached cloth.

shells and a "desert rose" of solidified sand has soft outlines and rhythmic lines which could easily be made into quilted designs. The snake, made into a large wall-hanging, could be fascinating instead of frightening if skilfully hung.

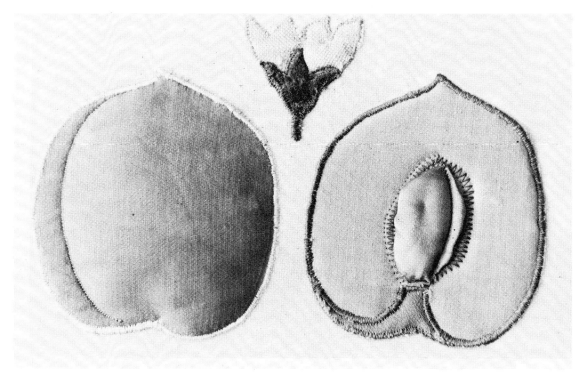

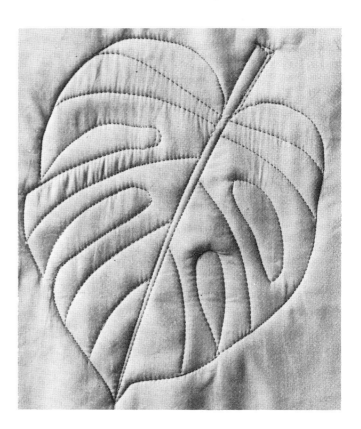

NATURALISTIC INTERPRETATIONS often involve experimenting with materials and techniques in order to discover different ways of achieving the required effects.

The incomplete lampshade shown on the left is made from grey-green organza over white silk and synthetic batting with cut-out leaves of thin corduroy laid in between, and bias-cut strips of the same material covering the hoops. The material produces a beautiful effect both when the lamp is on and when it is off. The idea is also suitable for partition screens and clothes.

Leaves made using the same materials as in the lampshade. Stems in very fine buttonhole-stitch.

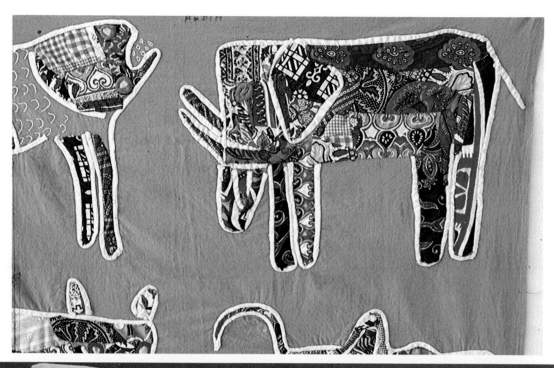

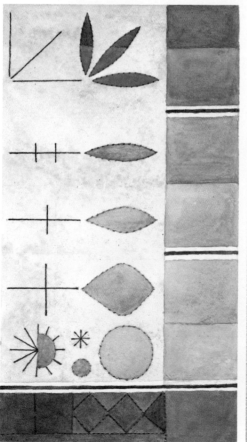

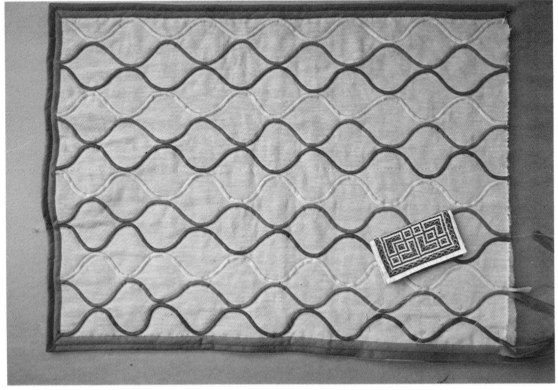

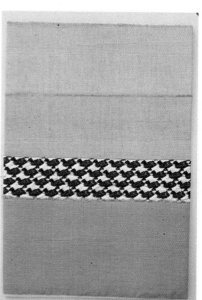

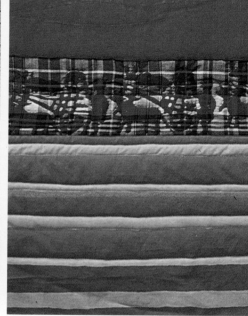

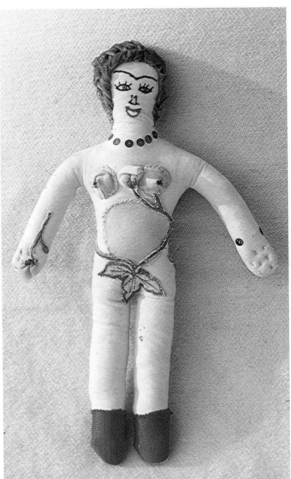

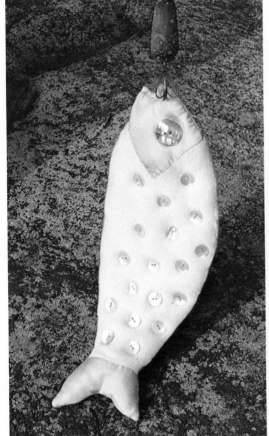

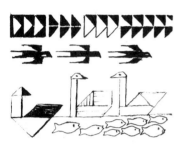

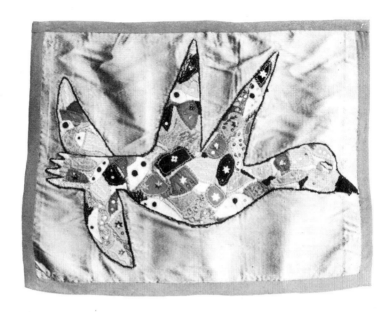

Very simplified flight of birds made up of triangles; more naturalistic sketches of swallows; swans made from patches; fish in either quilting or appliqué.

Woven fish motifs as the model for padded appliqué work on a handbag. Colour picture of the other side on p. 70.

BIRDS AND FISHES and their feathers and fins are rewarding subjects. You can take as your starting point either naturalistic pictures or simplifications such as are found in woven designs. The actual technique of weaving itself produces shapes suitable for both patchwork and appliqué work. Primitive peoples who live by hunting and fishing have, through their observations of nature, developed the ability to bring out character and movement in such pictures. The bird at top right is from Mexico, the fish below from Tunisia. The flying bird above shows how you can cover the surface within a shape with all manner of patches, embroidery, beads and sequins. Simple sketches taken from memory allow you to choose from a variety of solutions.

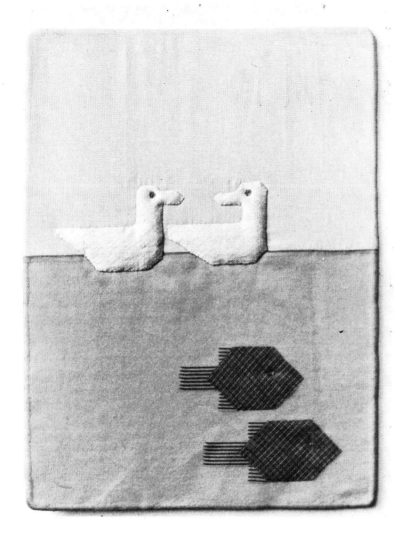

The padded birds look as if they are swimming on the surface of the water, and the fish as if they are seen through very clear water. The fish are placed below a layer of very thin material, which could also have covered the lower parts of the birds to give the viewer the sense of being below the surface of the water. The idea could be extended to aquaria, underwater scenes, etc. The facing material, in this case a single piece, was stretched on the frame together with a layer of felt before the rest of the work was begun.

The birds are made from shiny linen with a pattern which looks like feathers.

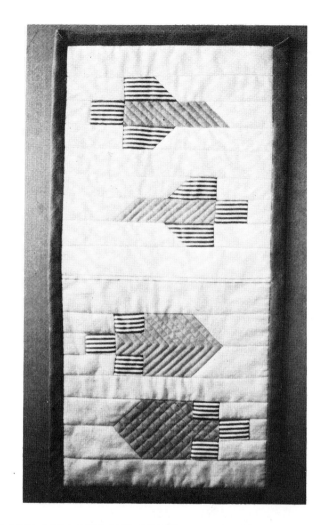

Birds and fish made of joined, straight-sided patches can be inserted between strips as at top right. Above a double-sided reflector tag in a similar style – like a little aeroplane.

CARS, BOATS AND AEROPLANES are suitable motifs for designs on cushions and bags for use in cars, boats or when travelling. The illustrations are in patchwork and appliqué work.

Another type of reversible pattern – cushions with car and boat designs. Quilting can be used for sails.

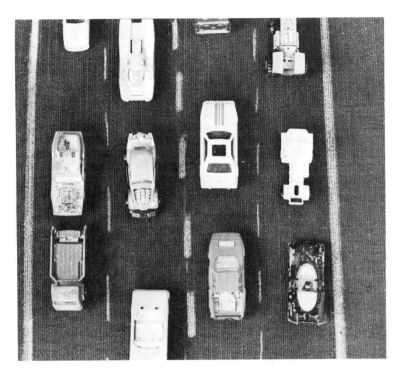

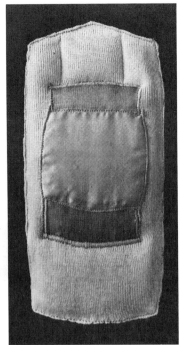

TRAFFIC Toy cars on a rug look rather like a photograph taken from a skyscraper. A suitable design motif for a wall-hanging in the home, or in nursery and infants' schools. Boats can be portrayed in a similar way.

Car from above – made experimentally by copying the illustration on the left.

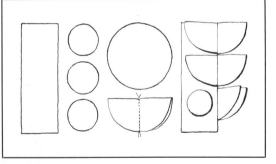

Traffic lights on a door used as a way of saying that you do not want to be disturbed. The cowls are also flaps that can be folded down to cover for example, the top two circles. Cut a rectangle and three large circles of black cloth; fold, fill and sew them together. Red, amber and green circles of velour, stretch terry-towelling or a similar material are filled and sewn into place. The black rectangle is here padded and sewn on to a larger board with a fabric covering, but it can be made freestanding.

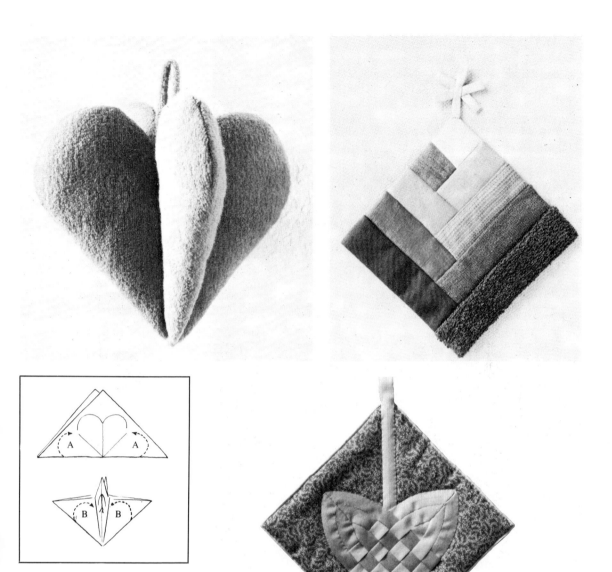

This soft, cuddly heart – which can also be used as a hanging decoration – is easy to make out of a square of red velour or terry-towelling. Fold the square diagonally in half and sew half circles (A) round templates. Fold along the other diagonal and sew the half circles (B). Leave a slit so that when the edges have been trimmed the heart can be turned right side out and the four compartments filled and separated by means of stitching. Fasten the loop on and sew up the slit.

HIGH DAYS AND HOLY DAYS

CHRISTMAS symbols such as fir trees, stars, hearts, gingerbread and Christmas crackers have shapes suitable for sewing in patchwork and appliqué work and then quilting, either for Christmas decorations or for more practical uses. They can be used to make pot-holders, bibs, wall-hangings, tablecloths or small items to give as presents. A stocking to fill with Christmas presents can also be quilted. See p. 141 for a design suitable for Advent.

A Christmas tree to hang on the wall takes up less space and can be rolled up and put away if – like this one – it is made from strong jersey with appliqué work and detachable decorations. The triangles are padded and sewn on with herringbone-stitch. Streamers are made of strips of cloth with threads pulled out. Reversible decorations of cloth, but paper would be just as good.

Hen and cock with different uses – she keeps eggs hot, he keeps bottles cool. The neck holds a wine bottle, the body beer bottles.

EASTER SYMBOLS Eggs and hens can be used for quilted egg cosies of various types, or as table decorations. They can also be used as translucent ornaments to hang in windows or near lamps, or to be hung in bunches of budding twigs in springtime.

Just a head – large for an egg basket, small for an egg-cup.

Against a strong light, a little egg shape on a white translucent egg can become a bird, or perhaps a fish. The "surprise" made from kitchen foil is placed inside the silk egg, which is padded to give it volume. Some types of filling can be pressed so that they taper off towards the edges.

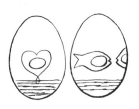

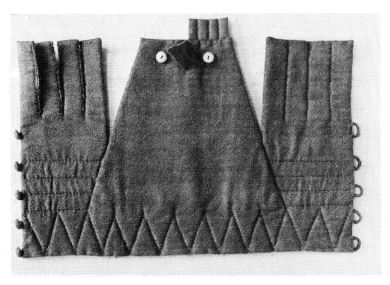

Flat hens that are easy to wash and store, made from terry-towelling, thin plastic foam and cotton lining, and fastened with press-fasteners or buttons along the back and the neck. The cockerel has stiffening material ironed on to the back of the comb and tail feathers.

"View from behind curtains" shows a simple alternative to a frame.

Maypole, either small or large enough to reach from the floor to ceiling, possibly on a transparent background. Here made of double corderory with batting in between, quilting to represent leaves and garlands of patchwork.

SUMMER SYMBOLS SUCH AS FLOWERS AND GARLANDS can become large or small quilted motifs, such as a picture of a window made as a wall-decoration, or a garland of flowers or a decorated maypole. Other possibilites are houses with flower borders, and puzzle-games made up of summery pictures. Try using them as a way of bringing the summer indoors to people who are unable to get out.

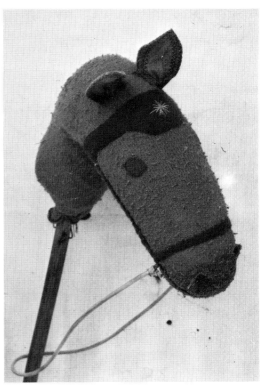

DOLLS AND PLAYTHINGS

NOT JUST TOYS Needlework representations of people and animals can be toys but can also be portraits of characters in literature which can be displayed or used in films and plays. An expressive doll may be the best type of photographic model if you want to convey a particular idea, and textile sculpture is becoming an increasingly common art-form.

The crown of a hat, quilted and filled and with a head and legs added to look like a beetle.

Sock padded to form a hobby-horse.

A flat doll with a large embroidered head, very easy to make.

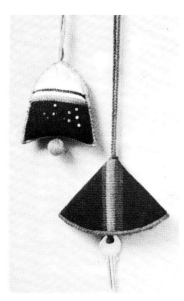

Velour and stretch terry-towelling roll naturally around strips of the same material or plastic foam. Sewn with concealed stitching.

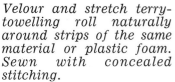

Padded key-holder with buttonhole-stitch round the hole for the neck cord to run through.

PLAYTHINGS AND USEFUL THINGS Try out different fillings. In the picture on p. 120, the black animals from Kenya contrast with the gingham pig inspired by Piglet in *Winnie the Pooh*. They are all tightly stuffed, probably with wool. The fish is of a knitted fabric with a very soft filling of synthetic batting. The mother-of-pearl buttons give it some weight and hold the filling in place. Other items shown on this page are a padded pincushion to hang around the neck; birds made from clothes pegs with wings sewn on and used, like pigeons, for carrying messages and reminders; an unfinished belt; and easily gripped playthings for babies.

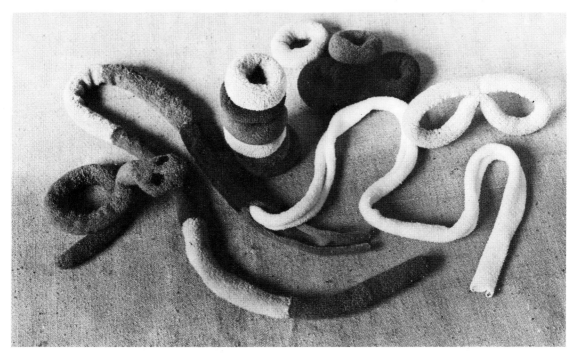

PEOPLE AND FASHIONS This hanging puzzle game for children has quilted squares with Velcro tape sewn on the backs, so that the figures can exchange sections of their bodies. This idea can be varied, using animals, for example. Instead of exchanging sections of their bodies, the dolls can exchange or change their clothes, like quilted versions of dressing dolls. Below, printed material in the style of the 1920s was used for the upper parts of these storage pockets for gloves and brushes. The pockets, made from folded suede samples, also look like clothes in the style of the period.

Two heads, sewn together with double batting in between, with narrow stem-stitch outlines. Could be used, for example, as the head of a puppet in a fashion show.

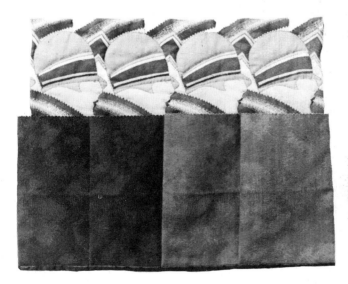

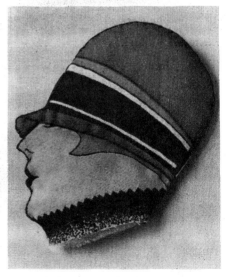

132

A child's drawing gave the idea for this mask, fastened on to a spectacles' frame. The eye-holes are held open by means of rolled-up cardboard. Because of the wired edge and the elasticity of the material, the shape and facial expression can be altered to some extent. The whites of the eyes are made of silk, the hair of frayed cloth.

FACES Hand-sewn masks. These table mats, pot-holders and glasses-cases were made to practise machine stitching with the grain of the top fabric and that of the backing laid in different directions to stop them pulling out of shape. The filling is felt or batting. Note the mouths like buttonholes, the dark glasses in appliqué work, and the frames and eyes in straight and zig-zag stitching. The quilting is, of course, the same on the reverse, but the cloth and the bottom thread can be in different colours. Children's drawings and book illustrations can serve as models, and the masks used by primitive people are an excellent source of inspiration for artistic treatment of volume, line and colour.

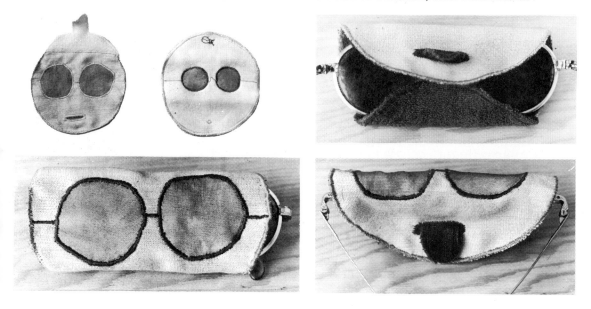

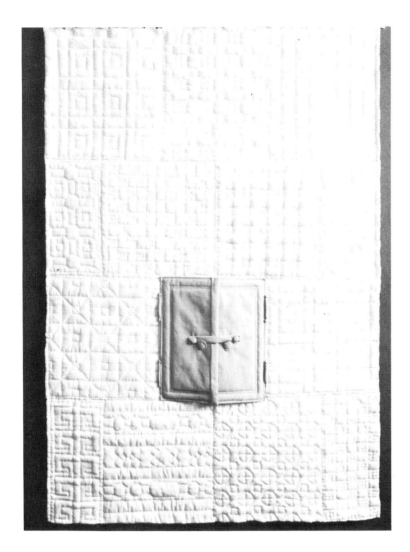

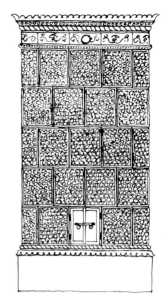

A quilt became a picture of a tiled stove by exchanging one block. Hand-quilted linen looks like the tiles used for such stoves. Firebox doors of brass-coloured satin with light synthetic batting in between. Can be opened to show the fire-box with flames of wrinkled silk.

DOORS, WINDOWS AND LIDS can be sewn on as if really hinged, on flat representations of houses, tiled stoves, cupboards, boxes etc. It is important to assess weights, sizes and strengths and to be sure that the backing will stand the strain. A wall-hanging such as a tiled stove, made as a group effort, can be a much appreciated reminder of how house interiors used to look. Patches of linen with a patterned weave have a very similar relief effect, when quilted, to that of old tiles. Quilting is also suitable for making cupboards and doors with various types of mouldings. Large wall-hangings showing windows and doors can have old-fashioned roller blinds and curtains that can be opened and closed. Decorations which also stimulate activity are of special value to the sick and the handicapped. A cupboard in appliqué work, for example, can open to reveal clothes, kitchen utensils, tools or toys, or it can be a dolls' house or a Christmas crib. Another possibility is an Advent calendar, complete with little doors.

Decorative picture or child's puzzle game in which the aim is to sort out objects found in the sky or the air, on land and in the water. The colour illustration on p. 72 shows how the colours give guidance.

A MINIATURE WORLD A wide variety of educational playthings can be made using textile materials. Here is a puzzle with a summer theme, which can also be sewn together and will then stand up as a three-dimensional work with a house in the middle, trees and animals all around, the sun in the sky and a boat on the water. It is sewn entirely by machine except for the quilting of the starry sky and the bias binding round the edge, which is stitched down by hand on to the reverse.

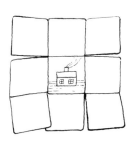

The corner squares can be left out or concealed behind other squares so that the "world" can be folded into a cube and fastened at the corners with Velcro or hooks.

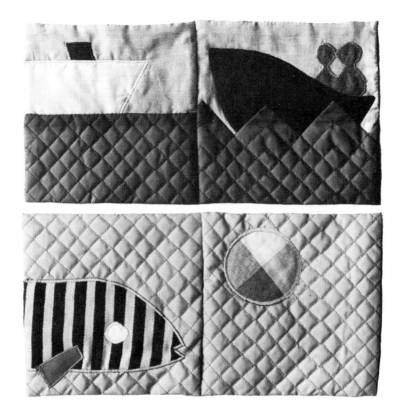

The material has a sheen which alters from dark to light according to the way the light falls on it.

QUILTED BOOKS Children love to turn pages and "read" like grown-ups. Why not sew a book with simple designs on one or both sides of each page? Choose a strong and easily washable material. I used thin, blue, quilted nylon lining material and let it represent water.

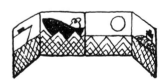

If they are not made reversible, these motifs can be used inside a cot or on the wall behind it.

The machine-quilting is oversewn with another colour to form the net that the fish are caught in.

A strip of this material 22cm × 120cm was divided into four. Each piece was folded so that the folded section came halfway up the piece, and the rest then represented the sky. The problem then was to find design motifs which were of the right shapes and sizes to correspond on both sides of a page. Pieces of material to represent the sky were put in place, and chimneys, houses and people were sewn on first; then the rest of each motif was sewn on with close zig-zag stitching. The patches on the fronts were pre-cut but those on the backs were trimmed afterwards close in to the stitching. The "water" was folded up and sewn in place, the edges sewn down and the pages then fastened together.

Squares sewn together either like accordion bellows or like books can be stood up to make little rooms. With

The method of quilting had left one of the selvedges of the material with a wavy edge. Folded up over the boat, this became high waves. The picture on the right is amusing, using the same shape for two different design motifs.

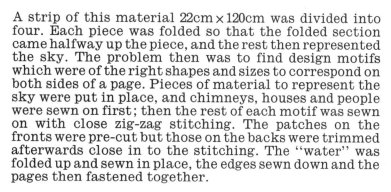

suitable design motifs and perhaps small doors and windows they can become amusing and educational playthings. If designed to form a cross they can show four different environments, four seasons, four times of day, four animals and the way they live, etc.

SYMBOLS AND SIGNS

Simple pictures, geometrical shapes, letters – different epochs and cultures have had symbols with particular meanings. These can be used as decorations, monograms or used on patches to mend holes. A cushion, pillow, handbag or pocket can be entirely covered with such a symbol. The letters need not always be particularly legible, and can be shaped more like patterns or images.

The word LOVE opposite consists of leaves, a flower, a bird and a heart, placed on Japanese silk above synthetic batting and a backing material. The whole surface is then covered with a very thin material and the quilting stitched round the shapes to hold them in place. If the material is apt to pull out of shape it is better to quilt right across them.

Musical notes are easy to sew in quilting and appliqué.

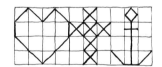

Charity – faith – hope.

Symbols for contrasts like sun-moon, waxing-waning, day-night, life-death, love-hate are often very simplified.

A heart in quilting, appliqué or as a filled, free-standing shape. The motif can be repeated over a surface or arranged in rows, and used to reinforce or mend.

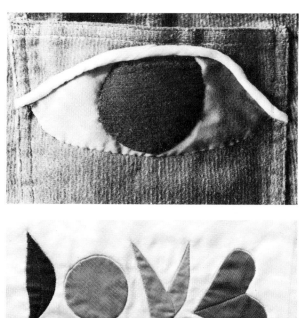

Music and record case.

SOFT LETTERS IN RELIEF both to look at and to touch. We interpret things we see with the help of shadow effects as raised, soft, smooth, rough, etc. The impression can be reinforced by feeling. A patch may be padded or have a different structure from the background material, e.g. terry-towelling, velvet, felt, leather, fur.

Baby's blanket made from cotton on terry-towelling with lettering sewn on.

Above, patches of soft wool with batting underneath.

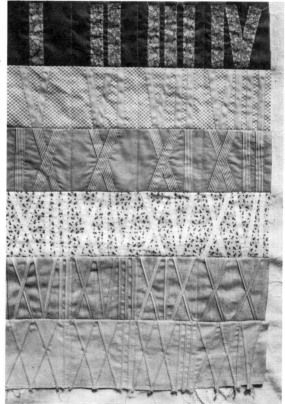

strips of cloth

bias binding

striped material

binding

bias binding folded double

braid

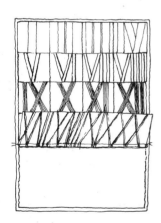

Advent decoration, shown in colour on p. 69. Row after row of appliqué, sewn on and folded down over synthetic batting on a firm backing, with vertical stitching between each date.

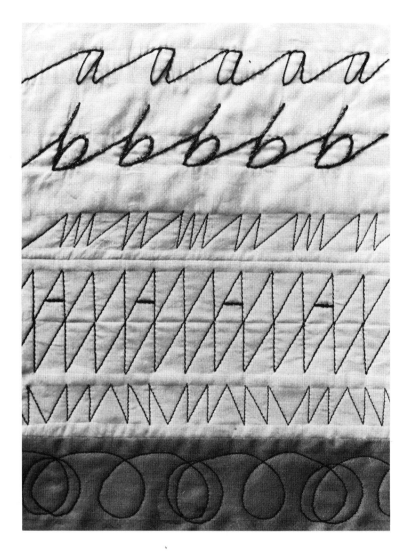

Stem-stitch with large daisy-stitch for each letter.

Stem-stitch in silk.

The remaining rows in machine stitching following lines marked out with a needle, some straight, some in circles. The cross-pieces of the As sewn afterwards. All on thin cotton and felt.

COHERENT LINES OF TEXT sewn by machine or by hand, may be used as quilting on belts, glasses-cases, handbags and so on. Above, the letters are repeated, but a message, a name or a date is more common. It may be handy and attractive to let the line remain continuous even between words but to increase the spacing. Arabic numbers usually stand alone, but Roman numerals are often connected by horizontal lines.

1234567890

Try embroidering the date, in either Arabic or Roman numerals. If the figures are small, use back-stitch, stem-stitch or chain-stitch.

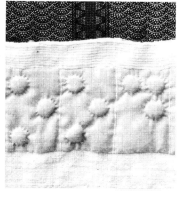

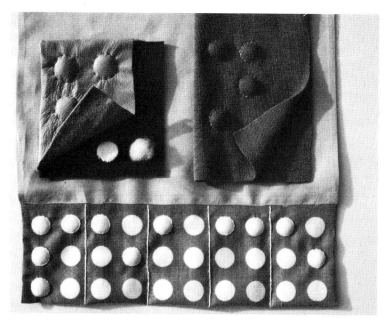

Detail from the blanket below and various examples of symbols stitched in leather, jersey and silk.

Soft cotton blanket with braille edging. A strip of synthetic batting below cotton. Circles in running-stitch marked out with small coins, drawn together by means of stitching from the underside.

BRAILLE The tactile value of quilted work, i.e. the way one understands form through the sense of touch, is particularly valuable for the visually handicapped. Quilting is admirably suited to braille. The raised dots, which also make a decorative pattern, are easy to produce. To be easily read, they should be no larger than the tip of a finger and be placed at the correct distances apart, see below.

If you find a spotted material in which the sizes and spacing of the dots are about right, it is easy to pad the dots which should be raised and to leave the others, creating in effect secret writing, see the border above.

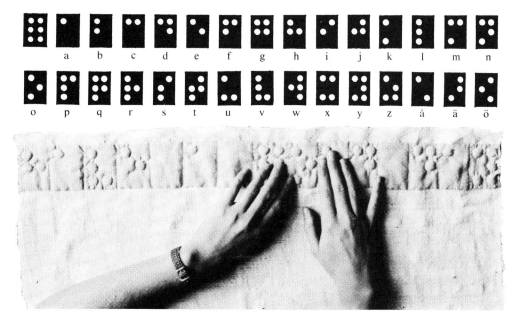

Index